FIVE POETS
PS508...

P9-AFP-330

)1

DATE DUE

AP 1 '94			
OC 6 '95			
APR 0			
MY 3 0 '96			
OC 28 '96			
DE 1 8 '03			
NO 15			

Five Poets
of Aztlán

Bilingual Press/Editorial Bilingüe

General Editor
Gary D. Keller

Managing Editor
Karen S. Van Hooft

Senior Editor
Mary M. Keller

Editorial Board
Juan Goytisolo
Francisco Jiménez
Eduardo Rivera
Severo Sarduy
Mario Vargas Llosa

Address
Bilingual Press
Box M, Campus Post Office
SUNY-Binghamton
Binghamton, New York 13901
(607) 724-9495

Five Poets
of Aztlán

Alfonso Rodríguez
El Huitlacoche
Leroy V. Quintana
Alma Villanueva
Carmen Tafolla

Edited by
Santiago Daydí-Tolson

Bilingual Press/Editorial Bilingüe
BINGHAMTON, NEW YORK

ISBN: 0-916950-41-7
Printed simultaneously in a softcover edition. ISBN: 0-916950-42-5

Library of Congress Catalog Card Number: 83-71140

PRINTED IN THE UNITED STATES OF AMERICA

Cover design by Christopher J. Bidlack

Photo credits: p. 60 by Tony Wu, Visual Impressions, Greeley, Colorado;
p. 94 by Randall G. Keller; p. 118 by San Vicente Photography, Silver
City, New Mexico; pp. 138 & 139 by Wilfredo Q. Castaño.

Acknowledgments

Several poems by El Huitlacoche first appeared in *The Bilingual Review/La
Revista Bilingüe:* "Searching for La Real Cosa," in Vol. V, Nos. 1 & 2 (1978);
"The Urban(e) Chicano's 76," in Vol. III, No. 3 (1976); "From the Heights of
Macho Bicho" and "¡Hostias!" in Vol. II, Nos. 1 & 2 (1975). "By Waterbug Be-
loved" appeared in *Hispanics in the United States: An Anthology of Creative
Literature,* ed. Gary D. Keller and Francisco Jiménez (Ypsilanti, MI: Bilingual
Press, 1980).

Poems by Carmen Tafolla that are included here have previously appeared in
Canto al pueblo. Arizona (Tucson: Post Litho Press, 1980); *Curandera* (San
Antonio: M&A Editions, 1983); *Canto al pueblo: An Anthology of Experiences,
1978,* eds. Leonardo Carillo et al. (San Antonio: Penca Books, 1978); *Get Your
Tortillas Together* (San Antonio: Rifán Press, 1976); *Washing the Cow's Skull*
(Fort Worth: Prickly Pear Press, 1981); *Cedar Rock* (San Marcos, Texas), Vol. 6,
No. 1 (1981); *Caracol* (San Antonio, Texas), Vol. 2, No. 2 (1975); *The Third
Woman* (Boston: Houghton-Mifflin, 1980); *Maize* (San Diego), Vol. 4, Nos. 3-4
(1981); *Women Working: Stories and Poems* (New York: McGraw Hill, 1979);
Album USA (Glenview, IL: Scott-Foresman, 1984); *Flor y Canto II* (Albuquer-
que: Pajarito Publications, 1979); and *Tejidos,* Vol. 4, No. 4 (1977).

Contents

Introduction

VOICES FROM THE LAND OF REEDS[1]

Santiago Daydí-Tolson

Five Poets in Perspective

Although only fifteen years have elapsed since the auspicious genesis of a Chicano Aztlán, there is already a surprisingly large and rich body of literature produced within the geographic boundaries of this symbolic nation.[2] Many and varied voices are coming from the Land of Reeds. Of these, those of the poets are the most numerous and diverse, perhaps because poetic language is best suited to expressing the generative forces unleashed by a people's renewed awareness of its common destiny.[3] The publication of poems in literary magazines, anthologies, and books by individual authors has been continuous and has created an equally sustained attention from readers and critics. Also, there is clear evidence in the number of periodical publications that deal with Chicano literary criticism of an ever-growing dialogue between critics and poets. Those interested in studying the poetry of Aztlán will find in the criticism devoted to it a well-defined set of characteristics and critical questions to work with and from which to advance new observations. This collective edition of five books of poetry written by five young, emerging Chicano writers proposes to add some new perspectives, critical as well as poetic, to the ongoing literary dialogue.

Each poet contributes to this edition a collection of poems, most of which are published here for the first time. Although the names of these five voices of Aztlán are not new among Chicano writers, they are not yet well known and deserve to be introduced to a wider public. Their poems are telling examples of today's developments in Chicano poetry and should be placed among the works of other contemporary writers, be they Chicano, other Latin American, or Anglo. It seems appropriate, then, not only to make their work available through this collective edition, but also to assess, from a critical perspective not necessarily limited to a Chicano point of view, the aesthetic value of their contributions to literature in general. This is why my critical attitude when examining their works has been not so much one of praise as an objective critical search for indisputable literary qualities. The mere fact that these five books have been collected here and given the critical attention of this edition should be indicative of the literary merits of their authors.

The poems speak for themselves, but a critical consideration of their characteristics will render their terms more meaningful, particularly in reference to the literary context in which they have been produced. An overview of the main critical ideas being discussed in relation to Chicano poetry precedes the comments on the individual poets and should serve as a background for a reading of the poetic texts as well as a basis for continued research and discussion in the field of Hispanic literature on the American continent. Of practical interest to critics, students, and the public in general, the annotated bibliography at the end of this volume complements the critical introduction, adding a summary of the most significant studies on Chicano poetry published to date.

The Wider Scope of Chicano Literature

The aims that define the criticism of Chicano literature today are summarized in the title of *The Identification and Analysis of Chicano Literature*,[4] a recent collection of articles that grapples with the basic preoccupations of critics of Chicano letters: the identifying of Chicano literature vis à vis the American cultural system, the search for its origins and background, its historical development, the critical views best suited to its study, and several critical applications analyzing individual authors or particular works. As a critic who approaches this literature from a Latin American perspective, I set myself the same objectives of identification and analysis, only situated within a wider context. My perspective incorporates Chicano literature into the scope of Latin American letters; that is to say, it views it as part of the continental literary discourse.

Some critics, often based in Departments of English, have set

Chicano literature, and rightly so, within the American literary mainstream, seeing it as an "alternate tradition."[5] Others have traced its relationships to Mexican literature as a natural consequence of cultural affinities and geographical proximity.[6] None that I know of has tried to provide evidence of the fact that Chicano writing, even that done totally in English, has a place among the Latin American literatures. Just a quick reference, for instance, to the similar approaches to the Indian past employed by Alurista and Ernesto Cardenal or to the generalized political commitment in both Aztlán and the more than twenty Latin American republics—and, alas!, dictatorships—provides indications pointing to a possible and necessary critical view that will open Chicano literature to the Latin American consciousness.

The inclusion—or intrusion, as some will prefer to say—of the American tradition in this ideal picture of a Spanish American community extending beyond national frontiers should not be a problem. Chicanos are, for all practical purposes, Americans, and there is no sense in trying to erase or minimize the consequences of this fact. On the other hand, there are many currents and undertows that make Latin American and American writing a relatively conjoint activity. Our histories are closely intertwined, painfully so in many instances. Today we are seeing our hopes, our fears, and our brotherly hatred running side by side in a competition that in its rudeness reminds me of those South American horse races where the riders not only aimed for the finish line but violently confronted their adversaries along the way. This circumstance affords Chicano literature the opportunity to become the link that will make for a still better relationship between the two extremes. Of course, this opportunity will come to fruition only if the literature of Aztlán becomes one with the literature of the Latin American nations.

The points of contact are many and insinuate themselves in innumerable ways. An epigraph to the first section of *The Identification and Analysis of Chicano Literature*, for example, was selected from Guillermo de Torre's *Claves de la literatura hispanoamericana*. Although there is no clear indication that the Chicano editor chose de Torre's words with the intention of tracing a relationship between both literatures, the coincidence of critical interests expressed by the selection of this particular text bespeaks the common grounds upon which to base the critical inquiry of both Chicano and Latin American literatures. It also suggests the need for future research that will include among the "keys" to Latin American literature the still-to-be-defined "claves de la literatura chicana." Some of these keys are already defined in the available criticism and should be reviewed and compared with their counterparts on the rest of the continent. There is still room to widen the scope of Chicano literary criticism, including in it questions and problems that would set it within the Latin American literary tradition.

The Identification of Chicano Voices

Foremost among the questions posed by Chicano literary criticism has been the identification of the national or group literature of Aztlán, an important task also confronted by Latin American critics in reference to their own nationalities. The difference between what was involved in the latter case and what is implied in this identification of Chicano letters is substantial, although not essential, and justifies a more intense dedication by concerned critics. The poets themselves give sufficient grounds for critics to decide whether or not such matters are central to their object of inquiry. In order to identify their own literature within any given culture, writers must first identify themselves and determine their uniqueness. In Latin America these identifications consist mostly of questionings that are clearly informed and delimited by recognizable historical, geographical, cultural, and political parameters. For Chicanos the inquiry is to be accomplished from within cultural, political and geographical boundaries that blend into the wider demarcation of Anglo America; in addition, Aztlanenses need the support of a strong conviction about their uniqueness even within wider sociocultural horizons.

The very existence of Chicano literature comes into question when trying to establish its demarcations. For those who have a personally experienced conviction about its existence, it might seem ludicrous to even think about ways to prove there is such a thing as a literature of Aztlán. The poems, so definitely set in a recognizably Chicano environment, are for them enough proof of an actual experience as well as its communication. Each poet as an individual in the community is a protagonist in an epic of reaffirmation of the self, of the pueblo, and of its views about the world. All of this the poet expresses in a language that artistically elaborates on the people's own common, everyday language. The poems adopt a code which reflects the linguistic strategies of Chicano society, including English-Spanish code-switching.[7] This is a fact commented upon by critics and indicative of an essential characteristic of Chicano lyric poetry: the poets talk about their own experience in the concrete world of Chicano social circumstances, and they do it in the language spoken there.[8]

But one can ask, as does professor Luis Leal, if it is possible to identify the existence of a given literature on the basis of an author's ethnic identity; after all, how does one determine if an author is a Chicano?[9] By changing the frame of reference from the authors to the poetic personae, the literary voices of the poems who characterize themselves as Chicanos, the answer seems at hand. And it will be a specifically literary answer instead of a sociological one, concretely textual instead of vaguely biographical. There is nothing more concrete about a poem than the voice of its speaker— it is there for everyone to hear and interpret. This method of identification is not only acceptable, but, moreover, it is the best suited in the case of Chicano poetry. It is the voices of Chicano poetry itself which make it identifiable.

The arguments most often used in determining the autonomous being of the literature of Aztlán are based on sociological, historical, ethnic, cultural, and even geographic determinants, either considered separately or in more or less convincing combinations. These determinants duly account for all the objectively measurable data that lie outside the literary text, and yet even then the result is less than clearly defined. The writers themselves can determine the boundaries of Chicano literature by the characterization of their own literary personae (a textual datum never considered by other disciplines) as concrete individuals who appear to belong to the culturally determined group. Their literature is defined by the voices of those who declare their cultural identity and make express and repeated reference to it in their discourse. It seems that for the time being the Chicano writer needs to stress Chicano identity, a fact that accounts for the well-defined poetic personae characteristic of Chicano poetry.

There are several obvious ways to characterize the poetic persona as a Chicano and there will be the opportunity later to comment on some of them when dealing with the individual texts in this volume. What matters now is to observe that whatever the means, it is possible that with time they will become subtler as poets both strive for a deeper understanding of their particularity and try to reach a wider readership. As it stands now, there are signs in critical writings of a growing weariness with strictly ethnic motives and a need for more universal values.[10] Some of these signs, as I will show later, are also evidenced in the poets here assembled. But only when poets can remain essentially Chicano without having to resort to any of the ready-made ethnic, cultural, or linguistic identifying traits—the easy contrivances or stale topoi, as it were—will it be possible to know which are the true defining elements of this particular literature. At the same time, only then will it be possible to talk about universality.

Historical Identity

This conflict between a culturally self-enclosed literature and universality has also been encountered by other Latin American writers as a consequence of their own cultural dependence. The origin of this issue in Latin American and Chicano literatures is found at the starting point of the process by which a consciousness of the national character grew among the people. This question of identity, a dominant subject in Chicano literature, as I have already observed, encompasses practically all the characteristics that define it. It presently continues to be of interest to both critics and creative writers, even among those who ask for a more universal perspective. The markedly sociological character of ethnic or national self-awareness has set in motion, from the beginning, a critical activity of identification fixed in historical and ethno-cultural points of view that are still important pa-rameters in Chicano criticism. Universalism, on the other hand, is gaining ground as the sense of identity becomes less problematic.[11]

In contrast to the historical considerations affecting the na-tional literatures of Latin America, which are structured by the division between colonial and independent times with rare atten-tion to the pre-Columbian period, a more complex situation is obtained for Chicano literature. Chicano literary criticism has to consider the important factor of the superimposition of more than two cultures and their fields of action, and this partly explains the different descriptions one finds of Chicano literary history, which vary from a wide view encompassing pre-Columbian and colonial manifestations, to a more limited one that sets its beginnings at the American annexation in 1848, to a still more limited conception that dates Chicano literature from the Chicano political awakening of the 1960s resulting from a resurgence of cultural identity.[12] Each view has its own valid reasons for support and is able to make for its tenets a convincing interpretation of historic truth. However, the goal of critical endeavor should not be the approval and support of any one of the historic views, but only the objective analysis of the several ideological patterns that explain the different interpretations. It is of utmost importance to have a complete understanding of the present attitudes toward the immediate past and toward the forces pointing into the future.

The past, present, and future of Chicano literature are seen in terms of a cultural continuum representing the different stages in the socio-political configuration of the Chicano people. For literary purposes, the self-awareness of this people became a *Chicano* phenomenon only when the term used now to name the people was adopted—out of a recognition of their differentiating identity—by those who up to that moment had been building up the strength to take such responsibility. What existed before that date should be seen only as an antecedent, a proto-history of Chicano literature of obvious interest as history. For the writers and readers of the early 1960s these documents of Hispanic life in the United States must have been virtually nonexistent. They will become more valuable for present and future generations only if research and study prove their lasting significance and are able to incorporate them as an authentically living heritage. Something of this sort has happened already with the oral and popular traditions.

To say that Chicano poetry begins with the first Hispanic writer to inhabit the American Southwest seems too extreme a definition, if somehow accurate from a strictly historical perspective. It reaffirms, of course, a long tradition that can easily be traced back to Spain itself via independent and colonial Mexico, thus tying Chicano literature to the rest of Latin America. It does not represent, however, valuable information for the actual "identification and analysis" of the phenomenon under study. There are other descriptions of more interest to the present-day poet and critic. These have to do with the origins defined as intrinsically related to the people as producers and consumers of their own literature. However, this position also is not totally free of danger. Under its light the oral tradition acquires great significance and even predominance over other forms of literature in the Mexican American community. An obvious consequence of stressing the popular foundations of literature is the moving of the critical aim away from literary matters to focus too much attention on anthropological research into folklore and popular culture.

Sociological Factors

Up to now it has seemed most appropriate to deal with sociocultural concomitants when discussing matters related to the artistic endeavors of Mexican Americans. The mere classification of themes and motives, not to mention linguistic considerations, leads to almost unavoidable culturalist points of view.[13] A telling example of the complexity of factors a critic tends to consider when working with a literature whose main characteristic has been established from the start by its differentiating ethnicity is offered by the volumes entitled *Hispanics in the United States: An Anthology of Creative Literature*.[14] An equally ethnic approach with similar objectives dictates the present collection of works by five poets of Aztlán. One of these objectives is to focus critical inquiry and public awareness and interest on one of the literary manifestations in the Americas that has been left aside—not necessarily forgotten, but reduced to its own cultural limits—because of its ethnic differentiation. It cannot escape one's attention that the expressions "American literature" and "Latin American literature" also refer to a characterization of literature in terms of national identification and cultural exclusiveness not too different from the ethnic view. Still, the treatment of Chicano literature by writers, critics, and the public seems to imply that in its particular case there are some unique differences.

In their introduction to *Hispanics in the United States* (Vol. I), Gary D. Keller and Francisco Jiménez explain that in their "attempt to determine some ordering themes for the manuscripts" that were to be included in the anthology, they devised eight headings under which to group them. These sections represent, in their words, "certain commonalities in United States Hispanic life and art" and "may even have some additional value as signposts in the pursuit of a vision of Hispanic life, art, and culture in the United States." Basing their organization of the first anthology on representative categories of Hispanic values, they devote a minimal part—only one of the eight sections—to a very few poems with a universal (or non-exclusively Hispanic) thematic. The remaining sections include poems and prose compositions dealing with customs, attitudes, and cultural values that could easily be found similarly organized in other texts conceived as introductions to Chicano cultural peculiarities. The sizable disparity between the purely aesthetic section and the rest of the classifying groups speaks for itself: the literature of the Hispanic peoples in the United States, and certainly so that of Chicanos, is very much inclined to treat themes and subjects decidedly ethnic in nature. Regardless of genre, style, language, ideology, or the sexual identity of the writer, this literature manifests itself in very specific and exclusive cultural terms that set it apart from other national literary traditions on the continent.

The fact that literature reflects the cultural background of the writer and in larger terms the whole cultural system of a people is something that probably few critics would want to discuss; but to infer from this generally accepted idea that each and every literary work will have to deal directly and specifically with the most characteristically differentiating cultural traits of the writer's world is to suggest that literature is little more than an aesthetically pleasing historical and social document to be used for purposes other than the intrinsically literary. Anyone who has read a few good writers will have to agree that if asked to determine the ethnic, cultural, or national background of a particular author, in many cases—too many to be mere coincidence—he or she will be incapable of doing it. This is not the case, though, when the writer under consideration is a Chicano. The five poets here presented are no exception to the rule. The reasons for this easy identification are obvious.

For one thing, Chicano writers are fully committed to their cultural identity and everything they write has direct bearing on their immediate world of experience. This is a fact observed by most of the critics. It accounts for much of the realist character of Chicano literature *and* for its dependence on traditional motives and mythifications.[15] The embodiment of these two seemingly opposed directions is the concept of Aztlán, which was born from both poetic and political designs.[16] Aztlán, the mythical nation of no boundaries outside the people's collective body; Aztlán, the concrete entity of a cohesive group aware of its existence. Although it correlates with the once Mexican Southwest, it is not strictly speaking a geographic territory, since Chicanos live all over the United States, nor is it a sovereign state. Yet Aztlán should count in a conceptual way among the youngest of independent nations, a

Latin American country of sorts. As such it asks from its writers, artists, and intellectuals their undivided interest and dedication. The literature of a new nation always tends to underline national values and to document the struggle for independence and cultural uniqueness. Besides being a spiritual nation with only a few years of existence, Aztlán also refers to an ancient people who, having found themselves discriminated against, had to keep a strong, if troubled, sense of identity and self-centeredness. When the time was right for their emergence as a group with a voice in managing their own destiny within the socio-political system of the United States, their literature was made ready to speak about their nature in unequivocal terms, in direct, realistic documentation of their existence. Novelty and tradition, a will for a future and the recognition of their past—two powerful forces in the emotional adoption of a patriotic view of history, society, and politics— inspire Chicano writers and imbue them with the will to talk about themselves and others as members of the common, ideal father- land.

But even if these two reasons—the newness of Aztlán and the strong sense of identity maintained throughout the years—were sufficient to explain the preference of Chicano literature for themes related directly to the experience of the Chicano people, there is still a sociological factor that by itself could have produced a similar literary development. Until recent times Mexican Ameri- cans have belonged mostly to the economically lower classes of blue collar workers and landless farmers. The socio-cultural configuration of this group by the time Aztlán took shape not only separated it from the main currents of American literature, but also from any form of literature that was not popular and intrinsically related to its own world. With certain exceptions such as Alurista, whose penchant for pre-Columbian genre is notable, the first Chicano writers—and I am using the term Chicano in reference only to those who became involved in the spiritual configuration of Aztlán—took as their models and as their authentic literary tradition the voice of the storyteller, the verses of old songs and lullabies, the narrative quality of the *corrido*, the ironic humor of popular jokes; and all these forms were expressed in the same oral, popular language, the only means of literary expression readily available to the lower classes from time immemorial.

The influence of the popular background in the configuration of Chicano poetry is such that even now, after a rapid development of poetic discourses from an initial programmatic, popular poetry toward a more refined artistic expression, the poets of today—if the ones here presented are indicative of the norm—still cannot part with it; moreover, they seem to cherish it and preserve it in their texts as a defining element of their poetic identity. The authenticity of this appropriation of an oral and popular tradition is undeniable: it does not function as a mere decorative reference to the ethnic past, as some nativist works used to do in other Latin American settings, but it exists as the poem itself—it constitutes its vision and its words. There is no denying that these Chicano poets belong in a tradition they cannot—if they ever wanted to—refuse.

Of the five poets included in this volume, none is totally free from popular influences. These range from the equation of basic Catholic symbolism with the human experience of the migrant worker in Alfonso Rodríguez' psalms to the adoption of everyday barrio language for poetic effect in the works of Carmen Tafolla and El Huitlacoche. Alma Villanueva, like Tafolla, develops the popular myth of "La Chingada," which has become a recurrent motive in the poetry of the Chicana.[17] El Huitlacoche and Leroy Quintana work with the voices and attitudes of popular figures who keep alive the traditional humorous sayings of the campesino and the street young. With the exception of Rodríguez, who strives for a strictly literary Spanish register, these poets manifest their dependence on popular identity primarily through language itself. Thus their compositions exemplify one of the distinctive characteristics of Chicano poetry—its language traits, particularly its strategies of English/Spanish usage.[18]

The Languages of Chicano Poetry

I do not intend to discuss here what has already been studied quite well by others.[19] Instead, I would like to consider the linguistic peculiarity of the poets anthologized here in relation to my contention that Chicano literature is one of the several national literatures of Latin America. When the poet resorts to using only one language—either Spanish or English—the argumentation of my case is highly simplified or practically untenable. A poet who writes in Spanish should have little difficulty in making himself accepted as a Latin American. Even if only in theory, the poems of Alfonso Rodríguez are properly Spanish American. On the other hand, a poet who writes mainly in English—as in the cases of Alma Villanueva and Leroy Quintana, who use very little Spanish and only in short expressions—would never be accepted as a Latin American writer if the classification of poetry were based on strictly linguistic criteria. As a matter of fact, probably the best argument against Chicano poetry being considered part of Latin American letters would be the one that uses language as the characterization of distinct national literatures. The same argument, I would like to point out, could be made, for the time being at least, against those who place Chicano poetry within American literary expression.

In other words, we find ourselves at the precise point where Chicano critics and writers must have been the day they began to wonder about their situation with respect to the United States and their Hispanic background. If we maintain that each literary tradition has its own language it will be impossible to talk about Latin American literature as a whole. All kinds of new distinctions will have to be devised in order to be precise. To the major classifications of Brazilian and Spanish American literature would have to be added more exclusive groupings such as francophone literature, which includes world views as disparate as the ones in Canada and in the Caribbean. On the other hand, and this is much more important for us, two Hispanic writers in the United States, one writing exclusively in English, the other in Spanish, would be placed in two different literary histories, even though the only differentiating factor would be the language they use. I am well aware that this is not a negligible difference; after all, poetry is made of language. But I do not think language should be used as the only determining factor in the identification of a given literature. If that were the case this volume would be impossible.

This is not the place to initiate a critical investigation of the many instances in history when writers have been faced with the decision to select one language among several to use in their poetic expression. Examples are abundant, and although they tease the critic with their many variations calling for a careful study, a few quick observations will have to suffice for the moment, and only as suggestions for deeper consideration. Spain offers two strikingly significant cases in lyric poetry: the use of Gallego-Portuguese as a poetic code—a choice indicative of a distinct concept of poetry as an art form—and the bilingual Hispano-Arabic *jarchas*, a manifestly literary product of a socio-political situation similar in certain respects to the present one in the American Southwest.

Spanish literary historians do not seem to doubt the pertinence of considering these examples as part of Spanish poetic tradition, language having little to do with their decision to put them in the cradle of the national literature. I would suggest that there was no hesitation in their decision because it was an assumed fact that the languages involved were acceptable forms of communication at the time, even though characterized by different socio-cultural circumstances. If Gallego-Portuguese was well known by lyric poets and their public, the bilingual code-switching of the *jarchas* must have been closer to the characteristics of daily language use among the people living in territories with extensive cultural mixture. One can assume that at the same time and at the same place other poets were writing only in Arabic, and still others in what we can here call Spanish.

The coexistence of two or more languages in the same territory will always lead to a mixing and switching of codes and to the preference for one code over the other for specific communicative situations. Latin America has known this phenomenon from the moment Cristóbal Colón (I deem it appropriate to always use his Spanish name) set foot on land and began to write down Indian terms to name what was for him a new reality. Only the overpowering socio-political superiority of the Spanish language prevented a proliferation of dialects and ultimately of different national languages in Spanish America. It could not prevent some measure of mixing and combination, which accounts for the regional peculiarities of present-day Spanish on the American continent. The Hispanic groups in the United States have developed markedly different forms due to the long influence of a superimposed language. That presently there is a linguistic code exclusively Chicano is an undeniable fact that justifies imagining a theoretical Chicano literature written in a language of its own, neither English nor Spanish, a literature at the same time American and Latin American—a link in the encounter of two worlds.

Bilingual code-switching is more than a stylistic device or a compositional characteristic of Chicano poetry.[20] To a great extent, bilingualism is the language of the Chicano poet, the very "stuff" poetry is made of. It is, then, as distinct a code as English, Spanish, or Portuguese, the main literary languages of the Americas. That it may be, unfortunately, a language of transition does not take away its right to be considered as a linguistic and poetic code capable of creating its own original expression. Latin Americans know what it means to gain for language the autonomy of a literary voice and the freedom to express oneself with all one's eloquence in this newly autonomous tongue and should recognize in the present-day Chicano creation of a poetic language a challenge similar to their own.

At this point in the historical development of Chicano literature the choices a writer has in matters of language are ample, as the present selection of five poets demonstrates. The two extremes, as indicated previously, are represented by Rodríguez' book, written solely in Spanish, and by the works of Quintana and Villanueva, written mostly in English. In the first case the adoption of Spanish bespeaks an almost exclusively Hispanic world view manifested also in the poetic imagery and a certain preference for traditional Spanish poetic composition. This type of poetry coincides with an earlier stage in Chicano tradition, one that originates in the nineteenth century as identifiably Chicano. It is still operating today and could possibly grow in importance and effectiveness in coming years. A certain weakness in the poetic voice, which deserves to be studied in order to define it properly, suggests the need for further experimentation among poets. As will be corroborated by Tafolla's case, it seems that Spanish used alone is still less expressive than English or code-switching as a means of communicating today's Chicano views and experiences.

At the other end of the language spectrum available to the Chicano writer, English resounds with all its poetic powers and expresses vividly its visions of reality. This perspective, maintained by Quintana and Villanueva, is distant from Rodríguez' world of Mexican migrant workers. It corresponds to a different sort of Chicano cultural identification. If Rodríguez' voice suggests a monolingual speaker, the bilingualism of these two poets is so minimal in their texts as to be virtually passive. English is their linguistic medium and certainly will continue to be the medium preferred by many Chicano poets. It seems questionable then that either Spanish or English will become the exclusive language of Chicano poetry.

For now, and I will not try to predict for how long, bilingualism as exemplified by the works of El Huitlacoche and Tafolla constitutes in my view the principal language of Chicano poetry. As stated before, this is the authentically Chicano language in its most popular form. The poetic personae (*el vato loco* and *la chuca*) of some compositions are truly Chicano figures, and their linguistic habits are the basis for bilingual code-switching in the texts. In a contemporary poetic manner these authors, as well as the ones who use only English, have adopted common, even vulgar everyday language, thus giving Chicano language the opportunity to be poetically acceptable and, conversely, to make poetry an expression of popular views and culturally exclusive values. But in both poets there is a preference for English as the basic code, with Spanish used sparingly, as must be the situation among most younger, less-educated people speaking freely in the streets of the barrios.

There are, then, sufficient indications of a predominance of English in Chicano poetry (and in a minor, alternative key, its cultivation purely in Spanish) as to doubt the feasibility of a lasting Chicano literature bilingually unique. But even then the texts already written in the bilingual mode constitute a body of literature that cannot be erased and that should be made known to non-Chicano readers and writers as a document that will always keep open the option for others to adopt its poetic code as a specifically literary language. Besides, as long as poets feel the need to express their human experience as Chicanos, the language they use will continue to be theirs alone, no matter how much of it is English or Spanish. On the other hand, one cannot avoid noting here another factor—that other need in every poet—that could change drastically the linguistic choice of Chicano poets: the reader, who has to know how to decode the language in which he is addressed. If this reader is to be found among English speakers the poet will naturally decide in favor of that language alone. Perhaps this phenomenon already affects poets like Gary Soto who have been swept into the literary mainstream of American letters. But then Chicano poetry will have definitely abandoned its popular origins, although not necessarily its essentially Chicano character.

Poetry and Pueblo

For all its popular background, the present-day Chicano poem is far removed from the oral origins that many like to impose on it as a sign of authenticity. The truth of the matter is, as I see it, that the popular influence must have been mostly ideal and only ethnically inspirational, rather than valid and instrumental in the configuration of a style. The latter had to be born in genuine

literary fashion, as befits the writers who created it and the means
of its conveyance to the public. Radio, television, and cinema
constitute today, in a way equivalent to the storytelling or public
poetry readings of yore, the primary and perhaps sole form of
aesthetic experience for the masses. One has only to think of the
ever-present signs of mass media predominance—the ubiquitous
portable radios, unceasingly talkative television images, larger-
than-life cinematic figures and actions—to realize that literature
exists as almost an alternate reality to the one experienced daily by
the great majority of people. The literature of Aztlán may well have
been born from the lower social strata as an expression of their
immediate interests and needs, but it does not belong there
anymore and certainly will never return to where it began.
Literature has its own field of action as art and its own limited
public which does not have to belong to the socioeconomically
defined land of Aztlán.

It is very unlikely that the novelists, poets, and essayists writing
the current Hispanic literature of the United States are addressing
their words to a reader who is other than a relative sophisticate.
Their readership consists mostly of middle-class, college-educated
individuals who, like the writers themselves, keep informed about
new publications and other literary developments. The image of
the mirror, already used by others in describing Chicano literature,
fits perfectly my description of the limited extension of poetry in
the larger framework of Chicano culture.[21] Poets work inside a
closely knit circle of self reflections; the mirror is very close to their
eyes. Contrary to what many critics will suppose, this is not at all a
wrong or disgraceful predicament for an artist. Writers do not need
to lean out of windows and shout the Truth to the four corners of a
busy world that will not listen to them anyway. Their ministry, if
they are to be seen in sacerdotal terms as some like to suggest, is
much better served in the soul-searching preoccupation with their
mirror images. Their social awareness need not lead them to
develop a programatic poetry. Their protestations against the
social system, their commitment to the struggle for justice among
the nations of the Third World[22]—characteristics that include
them among Latin American writers—are not outspokenly voiced
by larger-than-life poetic figures but by the private voices of
humble individuals, those poetic personae who think, feel, and
talk like common people, the people of Aztlán. For them there is no
political rhetoric, only everyday, sincere existential language.

Faced with the concrete facts about literary consumption in today's society, old-fashioned critics would probably deny their actuality; considering them a misinterpretation of reality, they would maintain their conviction that literature is as vital and present for the lower classes as the *cuentos* or popular jokes the poet so artfully imitates. Others, without a doubt, would blame American society for the situation and would accuse artists and intellectuals of unethical conduct because of their commitment to art and thought instead of to acts and propaganda. Again, still others would accept the facts as a natural and welcome consequence of their struggle for better socioeconomic conditions. Chicano writers, an admittedly small guild, together with their public, tiny though it may be, have either emerged from the educated classes in the first place or have evolved from a social situation of economic deprivation to a position of relative prosperity that has given them the opportunity to become better educated individuals. The limited access to literature is a situation that does not only describe the Chicano literary scene but also that of the rest of Latin America, to name only what is under our consideration. The differences and similarities are there to be studied and compared in what should become a sociology of Hispanic American literature as a whole.

The Chicano poet who has developed a more sophisticated view of literature after enjoying the increased availability of educational and professional opportunities, as is the case of the poets included in this volume,[23] has an acute sense of artistic responsibility that surpasses the purely political needs of a previous time. If poetry found a generating force in the political and social activism of some years ago, its present-day development needs to be powered by more subtle forces, not all of a social and political nature, but all truly ingrained in Chicano values. Many of these values are still embodied in the popular customs of the lower classes, and poets cannot but pay heed to their manifestations. Popularism becomes, then, an accepted term to describe their endeavors, and one has to take it as such with all its socio-political undertones.

More than ten years after the political birth of Aztlán there is still a pervasive sense of a common future in most of these poems. Personal pasts and presents are documents of a reality that needs to be surpassed, in some cases by denying it, in others by building upon it the dream of things to come. But there is no visible propaganda beaming its rays of truth from the poems of these five poets of Aztlán. What could be termed political in them is a sincere recognition of their Chicano identity and the consequent critical attitude toward the circumstances that make it difficult to contend with this identity.

As for the observation that the younger Chicano poets are looking for ways to bring universality to their works without losing contact with their ethnic roots, this is a matter that should not require too much discussion.[24] "Universality" is a treacherous word that can be interpreted in as many ways as one sees fit. I would not ask any poet, and much less a Chicano or a Latin American, who have enough troubles with which to keep occupied, to worry unnecessarily about a matter of this sort. The mere fact that Chicano poets are dealing sincerely with their own identity should be sufficient to lead them toward poetic visions and treatments that, being essentially theirs, will at the same time find a general response. And this, probably, is as much as one can expect from universality. As is natural, each of the five poets here collected follows a personal, distinct path in achieving this objective and develops an original body of work that deserves individualized attention, even if it is only to show that no general characterization of the poetry of Aztlán can explain the diversity of its many voices.

Alfonso Rodríguez

From the start, Alfonso Rodríguez' *Salmos para migrantes* raises several questions of semantic ambiguity that affect the reading and interpretation of his work as a Chicano text. At first glance the title of the book seems to have only one possible meaning—a collection of psalms for the migrant worker to sing in prayer. But if the preposition "para" is given the meaning "in praise of," the title receives a rather different interpretation. This other possible meaning appears to be the most accurate, despite its improbability in ordinary language usage, after one has verified that all the poems in the book are written, like most of the Biblical psalms, in a form of address directed to a second person singular, in this case the migrant worker. This rather involved reading of the title calls forth the implicit religious view that cannot be overlooked when analyzing Rodríguez' work.

Another semantic factor should be highlighted here. The Spanish word "migrante," taken from the English term referring to "migrant farm workers," does not necessarily express this meaning alone in the context of the book. In its general meaning of someone who migrates it can be seen as a symbol because of its synonimity with "caminante" (homo viator), widely used in Christian religious contexts. This traditional allegory of man makes even more acceptable the view of a migrant as someone to whom one addresses a psalm. Rodríguez enriches and updates the old and universal motive with the concrete human experience of the Mexican migrant laborer. The dedication of the book to the author's parents, two real migrant workers in the United States Southwest, serves this purpose and, conversely, transforms the concrete Chicano experience into a symbol of humankind. Moreover, it stresses the tone of sacred praise directed to a people whose lives are seen in a spiritualized and symbolic manner.

If the subjects of the praise are authentically Chicanos, the praiser also has to be a Chicano since he characterizes himself as a fellow migrant:

> Dejo que la mirada
> se pasee por las lejanías
> y te diviso a ti,
>   migrante hermano

However, the symbolic character of Rodríguez' poetry and the lack of direct references to the ethnic origin of the migrant in the poems make it difficult for the critic to assert the identification of both the speaker and the character. In another reference to his brotherhood with the migrant worker the word used to name both suggests a less restricted interpretation:

> Hermano pasajero:
>   el tiempo que vas dejando
>   atrás al caminar
> ya no te pertenece.

These two examples show the characteristic use of two levels of signification in Rodríguez' work. On one level the migrant farm laborer appears to be an actual Chicano field worker, for so the dedication at the beginning of the book and the few references to life in the fields lead one to conclude:

> la tierra y tú
> han sido quemados muchas veces
> de tantos salvajes menosprecios
> entre un viaje y otro viaje

habitas con ella íntimamente
después recoges sus frutos bien habidos
y sigues tu camino
hasta las otras pizcas

On a different plane, which includes less specific references to a concrete reality, the migrant is only someone who walks the roads in a mostly symbolic journey. Psalm V, with its repetition of the verse "... y sigues caminando" that begins and ends the poem, is a good example of the transposition by which Rodríguez, following a long tradition of poetic and theological discourses, transforms the actual concrete experience of his people into a purely spiritual action.

Life is a road, an existentialist perceiver of transient human nature would say; echoing Antonio Machado, Rodríguez writes:

Migrante:
conforme a la ley de todo caminante,
tu vida es no más pasar,
pasar como siempre pasas,
dejando huellas sin rostro,
por los llanos...

Life is a peregrination to an ultimate place of happiness, Christian imagery would teach; likewise, the poet talks about the promised land:

pero vuelves a la faena
que ya te sabes de memoria:
a duras penas lo levantas
y le infundes nueva vida
y sigues caminando
hacia tu tierra prometida...

With this triple set of meanings—the concrete reality of the Chicano migrant worker, the view of man as a wanderer, and the image of man as a pilgrim—Rodríguez tries to interpret Chicano life and its predicaments. As indicated before, this procedure gives to the Chicano experience the universality so much desired by those who feel the need to overcome the constraints of Chicano themes, and at the same time establishes the Chicano farmworker as the most representative symbol of man in his search for the ultimate good. No other human being embodies, as the migrant worker does, the plight of humanity.

The reference to "hope" in the dedication is another ambiguous image of utmost importance to the interpretation of the book. In one sense it is the theological virtue; in another hope is the source of strength for the working classes in search of economic betterment. Its presence in the poems is directly related to the conception of the migrant worker as a pilgrim in search of a promised land, not so much a glorious and spiritual one as a material and concretely human one. The relationship of this view with the utopian conceptions of a Kingdom of God on Earth, supported by a Latin American theology of liberation and some poets who cultivate this theme, is another example of the common interests of Chicano and Latin American poetry.[25] Hope also gives to the poetic voice the character needed for its identification as a prophet among his people. Although the book contains no allusions to any specific political ideology, these psalms are, in essence, a Chicano political statement.

Two images that are constantly used in these poems are basic to this representation of the search for betterment: the road, in the ancient sense of walking path, and the representation of the passage of time, either through the different hours of the day or through the action of walking down the road. The ever-present image of walking forward embodies human temporality with its feelings of fleetingness and desires of perpetuation that surpass individuality to encompass a sense of history:

> ¿En qué momento pasa el instante
> a ser recuerdo?
> ¿En qué momento
> pasan tus palpitaciones
> a la historia?

This same sense of history underlines the individual's fear of total disappearance, of having lived for nothing:

> Migrante caminante
> eres como fantasma
> empolvado en el camino
> tu vida es no más pasar...
> pasar... y siempre pasar...
> pero... ¿quién verá las huellas
> de todo ese caminar?

The cosmic cycle of time is particularly evident to the farm-worker, whose life is regulated by the seasons and the rhythm of day and night. The succession of moments is thus a repeated

technique to stress the passing of time. The road itself is a measure
of time. The migrant worker knows, then, as no other creature
could know, the substance of temporality. The ancestral past, a
Chicano motive, is kept alive in the migrant's wandering from
field to field, from day to day, in a ritualized present aimed toward a
perfect future. The rhythmic repetition of the same stanza in Psalm
XV reproduces this ritual of hope:

> mientras tú pasas
> como ancestro viviente
> hacia otra tierra...

The migrant hopes for permanence even in the knowledge of
being a wanderer because such a state of fulfillment will have to
come. At both extremes of the temporal and spatial line concretized
in the image of the road one feels the presence of a static realm: a
Paradise of sorts. The original one, lost to mankind, is the land of
the ancestors lost to the Chicano people; the ultimate one,
triumphantly set at the end of the journey, is promised on the
individual level by God and on the communal level by God and
political visionaries. The Chicano migrant worker does not roam
the land in desperate search of a job but sets out on a journey that
will take him to the utopian land of justice:

> por ahora ese es tu privilegio
> tu sola recompensa
> pero llegará el día
> y ya se acerca
> en que un vástago retoñará
> de las raíces de la tierra
> trayendo en su cintura la justicia
> y acontecerá también en aquel día
> que sobre toda la faz de la tierra
> se cumplirán las promesas antiguas

The imagery is political and religious with clear allusions to an
ethnic mythical past. Two epigraphs at the beginning of the book,
a citation from a poem by Antonio Machado and a text from the
Bible, confirm the religious inspiration of these texts and suggest a
particular way of reading them. It would be erroneous to disregard
this information and read these psalms as devoid of their Christian
concepts. It should not be a surprise to anyone that only in such a
reading does the Chicano world view find full recognition of its
universality. No one would dare say that these *Salmos para
migrantes* are to be read only in terms of the Chicano experience.

Although they do spring from it, they surpass its specificity to become a symbolic text for a wider readership. The contention that this public is Hispanic rests on the rhetorical register selected by the poet—the traditionally Hispanic attitude, language, motives, symbols, and poetic techniques that include comparisons, images, anaphoric composition, and irregular combinations of basic metric patterns.

El Huitlacoche

El Huitlacoche writes in a totally opposite register as he brings to poetry not only a different attitude but also a very different language. Following a more contemporary feeling for the voices that appear in a lyrical text, El Huitlacoche sets as one of his objectives the characterization of the actual speaker, the *vato loco* and *pueta*. The fact that the poet does not use his own name or even a regular nom de plume but a peculiarly Chicano alias is in itself a very helpful detail in the characterization of the poetic persona; this is particularly true when the same alias is used by the poet to identify the speaker in some of the poems, and by extension in all the selections, including "El Huitlacoche's respectful translation" of Sem Tob's *Proverbios morales*. Someone who is known by the name of El Huitlacoche, who talks the way he talks and thinks the way he thinks, can only be an individual of a very specific ethnic and social extraction. As the poet himself puts it: "Pues, I am just a vato loco man," or, in a phrase surrounded by ironic observations, "the Hispanic father," the mature version of the street-wise youth.

If in the case of Alfonso Rodríguez it was necessary to allude to the religious background in order to obtain a correct reading and interpretation of his book, the most effective point of view for approaching El Huitlacoche's poems is to first highlight the role of the interlocutor, which might or might not be the same as the role of the reader. The use of the first person plural combined with the address to a second person helps create the sense of brotherhood so important for the effectiveness of these poems. The interlocutor in many of the compositions is another Chicano who is as ready as the speaker to laugh and criticize the circumstances of both the poet and the listener in overtly irreverent language:

> De mi parte
> como pueta
> tell US marines

> que aquí 'stamos nomás
> a las alturas
> de las circunstancias

The same objective of carnalismo is reached when the pueta directs
a rhetorical question to a listener he has captivated with a direct
call:

> Just one second!
> Isn't the three-in-one concept
> a very fine steak sauce?

and even more so when he uses a popular form of friendly address
both in Spanish and English: "forget it hombre," and "Let it die,
man." That he applies the same form of expression to Bobby K.,
lying on a kitchen floor in L.A. is also indicative of the socio-
political standing of the poet as a Chicano from the barrio. El
Huitlacoche's love poems are addressed to a woman who only once
is characterized as a Chicana when she talks to him in the typical
bilingual code switching used among the people of Aztlán: "¿Qué
pasa, Huitla? she asks / Got a bug up your ass?" Although not
precisely a love poem, "Rhetoric de la chingada" can only be
addressed to a Chicana.

This characterization of the speaker as purely Chicano, which
is accomplished by expressed attitudes and language usage, as well
as the creation of a fictional listener by means of a selection of
pronouns and forms of address that indicate a concrete act of
communication, create a general impression of the popular orality
so characteristic of Chicano poetry. The cultural antecedent of a
humorous and sharp-tongued public poet from the barrio is not to
be discarded—it is essential to the existence of this poetry. In most
of his compositions El Huitlacoche talks from the heart of the
barrio, from the same corner or bar where street-wise young men
get together just to talk, to let their frustrations and hopes express
themselves in ingenious jokes and word plays rarely free of sexual
references. Even the poems with less public interest maintain in the
context of the collection the feeling of communal experience
through the unity of the speaker's voice and the identity of the
implied readers. The nearer the actual reader gets to the suggested
socio-cultural situation, the better will be the understanding and
enjoyment of the text.

But there is always the possibility—an infelicitous one—of

taking the position of detached observer—that of the curious anthropologist or other social scientist—and reading this work as a quaint cultural document, engaging for some, minimally interesting for others. Precisely, the obvious danger for a poetry like El Huitlacoche's is the loss of its aesthetic appreciation because of the markedly ethnic nature of the poetic code in which it is written. Although extremely well composed and the result of careful and serious writing El Huitlacoche's work runs the risk of being misunderstood and consequently discarded for a supposedly unredeemable lack of universality, that magic literary quality everyone wishes to find in poetry and looks for in philosophical platitudes. Regardless of the future effectiveness and fate of this poetry, which depend only on the will of the public to accept it as meaningful artistic language, I would like to underline its poignancy as a Latin American text. In its historical and cultural foundations and its stylistic techniques El Huitlacoche's discourse reaches important aspects of reality that even the most obsessed universalist would have to accept as perfectly universal.

Let us consider once more the figure of the poet as conveyed in his language, attitude, and interests. He is, after all, the central factor in the structure of the work, not solely because of basic literary considerations, but also because he incarnates a human type that represents not so much an individual personality as an attitude of a whole group. Even though he is a lower class Chicano socioeconomically, his group identity includes all Hispanic proletarians in the United States and the rest of the continent. The dedication of one poem "Pa' don Pablo Neruda" is an invitation to understand its criticism of American military intervention as a continental call for unity among Hispanic peoples. The political ideology of the poet chosen to be a leading and inspiring figure is less important than the fact that Neruda represents, better than others, the common destiny of the Hispanic American nations and communities. The epigraph to another poem, taken from *Figuraciones en el mes de marzo*, a novel by the Puerto Rican Emilio Díaz Valcárcel, as well as the inclusion in the poem of scattered words from Puerto Rican Spanish signify the recognition of a Hispanic community in the United States wider than the one formed by Chicanos alone. The very Chicano concept of carnalismo has been extended to others, as has occurred among other Mexican American authors after the accomplishment of the first political objectives of La Causa. A similar extension to other Third World groups

can also be stressed in Rodríguez' final utopian view of a better
world for those who are still searching.

But what for many readers is a purely political theme, a
common one among Chicano poets, for the ideal reader of El
Huitlacoche's poems—the fictional listener, another vato loco like
the speaker himself—not only encompasses political meanings but
also discloses a whole concept of reality. The title of one
composition, "Searching for La Real Cosa," would suffice as an
expression of the existential anguish and the desire for human
fulfillment behind the political quest for social justice. The poem
develops its subject in a richly complex combination of voices,
linguistic registers, word play, and motives that capture the pathos
of a human search for identity in an inimical society.

Two verses in Spanish begin this composition. They reappear
several times, in variable form and position relative to each other,
throughout the poem. They set the tone for the whole composition
following the pattern established by the epigraph—a combination
of joke and serious need for an answer. There could not be a better
basis for a poem that plunges so decidedly into a subject that is easy
to dramatize to an extreme. Humor, as happens in daily life, is a
means to avoid lacrimosity and to unleash the most deeply felt
worries and complaints without sounding badly hurt. The true
feeling is voiced only in the second verse, the first being a funny
allusion to the quest:

> ¿Quién es La Real Cosa?
> ¡Dime, dime por favor!

The function of these verses and their repetitions in the poem is
to alternate a growing dramatic urgency for and despair of an
answer with the ironic and even saucy attitude expressed in the
intervening verses and short prose commentaries. Both verses and
prose make fun of the different members of La Raza and their ways
of dealing with identity. It is a self mockery that applies to El
Huitlacoche himself in the accusing verses following one of the
desperate questions that unify the poem with piercing insistence:

> ¡Dime, dime por amor de Dios!
> Poor Huitlacito
> Something's awry in his head.
> He does not take la Tequila
> He prefers Johnny Walker instead.

The confusing encounter of two cultural systems is concretized by the language used as well as by direct criticism of the social circumstances that perpetuate the situation. Bilingualism is used ingeniously to produce the funny and telling word play analogous to the speaker's characterization as well as the images of duality. A particularly significant word play that does not include bilingual use but refers to it is found at the end of the poem, when El Huitlacoche innocently declares his identity:

> I'm just a cunning lingual
> I no got stereoscopic vision

"Stereoscopic vision" makes direct reference to a previous section of the poem that criticizes the condescending attitude of Anglo society toward bilingual Hispanics. The final verses of that section are almost identical to the ending of the poem:

> I'm only bilingual
> I don't got double vision

The play on words alluding to a sexual act when associated with the final verses provides a joining of the linguistic motif with the sexual one, abundantly represented in the prose sections, which have the appearance of "notes" to the text of the poem. These include a series of topics ranging from the commentary about "hijo de la chingada" to a pseudo-scientific interest in the phoneme ch and its uses, mostly for sexual terms, in Chicano Spanish. The last of these sections closes with an ironic comment that hints at an interpretation of the many references to sex and language, and, particularly, of the penultimate stanza of the poem: "¡Charamba! I guess that just about sums up the notion of Chicano semantic fields!"

Sexuality, or better yet the verbal overflowing of sexual terms, is nothing but an exercise in language magic or exorcism and constitutes, as much as other data, an excellent comment on the Chicano world view. This attitude toward language gives away the Chicano identity of El Huitlacoche, especially if one takes into consideration that there are two essentially Mexican linguistic taboos active in his poetry.[26] One is the sexual taboo, clearly related to language and the sense of identification; the other is the religious one, manifested in several compositions, of which "¡Hostias!" is an excellent example because of its irreverently funny play on words and the dualistic meaning of the title, the only bilingual aspect of the poem. If I had to select an image indicative of El Huitlacoche's poetry, none would seem more appropriate than life in the barrio; more than the visual aspect of it I would stress the musical free flow of words in different social encounters, and above all the ironic laughter.

Leroy V. Quintana

Leroy V. Quintana's book of short poems can be described with a much used image, slightly changed to apply exactly to the particular qualities of his poetry. *The Reason People Don't Like Chicanos* is very much like one of those two sided mirrors, one side reflecting, in sharp focus, miniature, brief images of the G.I. experience in Vietnam, the other enlarging to a comic exaggeration scenes and characters from everyday life in a Chicano community. As in the two-sided mirror, the small round frame tightens restrictedly around the subject and focuses all attention on the bright, different-from-life, reflected image. There is no room in these compositions for digressions or elaborations beyond the minimum requirement for the briefest possible verbal conveyance of the scene.

Another similarity with the mirror is that the poems are reflections rather than the real thing; reflections of a past or of situations not seen or experienced directly by the speaker. In this respect they could also be compared with snapshots captured by a piercing lens, the almost irreverent eye of an observer who sees things in a different light and makes evident their twisted deformations. It would not be totally irrelevant to bring to mind here the model of traditional epigrammatic poetry—brief, sharp, critical, and ironic, always rendering the figure of a poetic narrator who has reached, through experience and disillusionment, a state of superior wisdom, expressed only by a half-humorous, half-sour twist of the mouth. The reader senses, almost sees, the presence of this man who, at the same time that he tries to have a laugh at reality, feels deeply moved by it and wishes it were different, even if only slightly different. Because life does not look that bad after all.

A final point of comparison could be the album of voices in Edgar Lee Masters' *Spoon River Anthology*. Brevity, exactness, and incisiveness; variety of characters, detachment with a slight touch of affection, and past memories are some of the similarities between the works of the aforementioned American and Chicano poets. Language is another. English in its common and simplest form, devoid of metaphoric and even acoustic embellishments, becomes the means of communicating the concretely human experiences of common people. As Chicanos, Quintana's characters use their native language, but the poet reduces it to a few words only to add to the spirited detail. Rhythm and timing are basic to the effect of these poems and Quintana cares for the *mot juste*, the correct twist of phrase. Spanish cannot become too obtrusive, otherwise it would interfere with the basically English metrics of the compositions. Other poets who use a combination of English and Spanish do not generally work with poems as short as these; longer compositions allow them more freedom to handle looser rhythmic patterns in which English and Spanish prosodic elements intermingle without badly hurting each other.

Quintana is a master of nuances and likes to avoid the overly manifest in favor of the suggestive touch or almost invisible sharp edges, sometimes all the more eloquent for their lingering effect. Observe, for instance, the use of Spanish in these verses:

> Says he surprises his wife from behind
> and kneads her nalgas
> the way she does the dough

Significantly enough, the Spanish word not only belongs to a very specific semantic field, but also adds an acoustic play causing both an alliteration and a surprise clashing of the Spanish open vowels with the English which comes before. A few other similar cases of brief intercalation of Spanish in a purely English text demonstrate that Quintana's use of bilingual code-switching is very restrained and resembles more a literary technique than the seemingly spontaneous use of a particular linguistic code, as happens among other Chicano poets.

Again, turning the analysis to the figure of the poetic narrator should give us another vantage point for explaining Quintana's particular use of language. Each section of the book, that is to say, each side of the mirror, faces a different environment, this in turn accounting for the different attitudes of the speaker in each case. I would like to believe that there is only one voice doing all the talking, although there is no way to support my contention except for the fact that both groups of poems have been collected in one book. The voice that speaks all of the poems belongs to a young

Chicano, one who was born in the barrio, was raised there among his people, attended American schools, and in due time was sent to Vietnam. In both groups of poems the persona is talking to someone who, like himself, is a Chicano, but who has not experienced the war. This is why there are two different techniques or focuses, one for each section.

In one case the concave crystal brings into perfect focus the very concise scenes of life in Vietnam. The use of the first person in some poems is the closest there is in these examples to a personal involvement by the speaker. There is only one example of the singular pronoun, but it is really related to a commentary about the disgrace of another soldier and the group. The individual appears only to express his compassion for his fellow men:

> I felt sorry for him
> and for the rest of us,
> as long after lights out
> we began crossing out days.

The plural pronoun stresses the feeling of comradeship, the common predicament, a sort of carnalismo that surpasses ethnic barriers to embrace all men suffering from the same experience of war. Thus, most of the time the speaker talks about others, individually or in a group, never about himself.

This selflessness, characteristic of Quintana, is not far from charity or agape, as in the case of the verses just cited or the last line of a poem about an Anglo soldier: "The war saddened his solemn eyes forever." On the other hand, and perhaps because of his capacity for compassion, the personal detachment works as a pointer to the strong feelings of disgust toward war and of pity for the men who have been sent to it as impersonal soldiers, mere victims to the slaughterhouse.

What happens to others is narrated in mean and cold terms, showing no evidence of compassion for their tragedies. This is the case with the poem about the death of a lieutenant, in which the neatness of the officer's apparel and the ugliness of death in a pit of rusted nails and broken bottles are cruelly contrasted. The poem ends in two short verses made sharply rhythmic by their caesurae and acoustically harsh by the combination of consonants:

> his fine, rigid body
> died a dirt-cheap, uncombed death

This composition can also be read as social criticism, a sort of getting even with the higher officer from a higher social class. Other poems that talk about simple soldiers are perhaps less sardonic, although they are still ironic, particularly when some criticism is implied. This general attitude of disdain and emotional detachment is very well expressed in the verse that the poet selected as subtitle for that section: "What Can They Do, Send Us To The Nam?"

Just as there are no long poems, neither are there large scenes of war, nor crowds or battlefield expanses open to heroic deeds. Nothing that does not fit inside the reduced frame of the reflecting surface can be reproduced, nothing that cannot be seen at an arm's length matters at all; to make out something in the mirror one has to get near enough to almost see it fog over with one's own breath. Likewise, the volume of the voice telling these moments of human misery is low and demands nearness in order to be able to detect it at all. No matter how the poems are read—silently or aloud—the impression will be always that of someone talking in the confinement of a reduced group, where there is no need to talk louder. The speaker finds himself among others remembering in almost joking terms past experiences he wants to exorcise by means of ironic comments. As if he did not want to talk about his feelings, he is quick and affectedly unemotional.

In this section on Vietnam there are no Spanish words whatsoever, no direct references to the Chicano world. On the contrary, all the characters depicted here are presented as Anglo Americans, either because their names and military ranks portray them as such, because they are given Anglo names like Combat Smith or Cookie, or because they are catalogued as Americans through indirect characterization—a soldier can assemble a gun "with the same ease as playing Yankee Doodle . . . " on his guitar— or simply because there is no indication one way or the other. War makes all equal, all victims of the system, the Anglo as well as the Hispanic. Any explicit allusion to Chicano reality would have been uncalled for here. It is sufficient that the speaker can be recognized as Chicano in the context of the book. There being no other means of characterizing him ethnically, it is to be assumed a tacit recognition of the fact that Chicanos are Americans.

The same poetic persona shows a different mood in the section devoted to his Chicano experience. This takes place in the enclosed

circle of a small town with its grocery store, its gas station, its old
bridge, and its typical characters—Don José Mentiras, Doña
María, and a few others who include an Anglo shopkeeper and the
speaker himself as boy and teenager. Caricature is not the best term
to describe the treatment of reality in these poems, but some of its
deforming traits are clearly put to use for poetic purposes. Life is
seen mostly on its funny side. Again, as in the poems on Vietnam,
the humorous attitude in most cases is ironic; in others it hides the
speaker's deep concern for what is being remembered or commented. In both circumstances it is a form of defense, a hiding of
the true feelings, as if showing them would be an undesirable trait.
This attitude, as in El Huitlacoche, is indicative of the poet's
ability to capture an important aspect of popular culture among
his people.

Spanish, then, becomes an important factor in the naming of
the world, but it does not come straight from the mouth of the
speaker—it belongs only in the words of others, mainly older
people. The most important among them is Don José Mentiras, an
old man who represents long-standing tradition among campesinos. Even his name has a folkloric tone that reminds one of a
Pedro Urdemales type of figure, a traditional character in Hispanic
folktales that tell of his ingenuity, popular knowledge, and ability
to lie and to talk craftily. The poetic persona is only a conveyor of
what José Mentiras has said. To do this he employs the same
pattern used for popular sayings attributed to some old man who
knows best because he has lived longer and seen more of the world:

> José Mentiras says that a Chicano
> sometimes has to do a lot of walking backwards
> in order to go forward

This narrative technique is in keeping with the personal
detachment of Quintana's poetic persona. From his position of
observer the poet merely points to facts and people that seen from
his perspective acquire representative and significant values.
Friendship, images of boyhood and the barrio, references to the
opposed realities of the Chicano and Anglo worlds, allusions to the
Americanization of some Chicanos, to racism and social injustice,
comments on love and on women's good sense are several of the
typical themes that Quintana treats as glimpses of reality in these

poems. They make a truly Chicano poet of his poetic persona, even if the language he uses is English.

Alma Villanueva

English is also Alma Villanueva's language, although she chose Spanish—Mexican Spanish, to be precise—for the title of her poem: *La Chingada*. Even in English her voice sounds unmistakably Chicana, partly because of the title itself, partly because of the attitude of the speaker and the substance of her words, which are distinctive characteristics of Chicana poetry. Alma Villanueva's writing represents, in effect, one of the main efforts among Chicanas to reproduce a feminist literary discourse in response to women's own questioning of their circumstances in Aztlán.[27] It is highly significant in this context that the translation of her poem into Spanish is the work of the poet's own mother.

If one remembers that the expression for "native language" in Spanish can be translated literally as "mother tongue," the subtle correspondences between the main subject of the poem, the sparse use of Spanish in it, and its translation to the language of the poet's mother appear as more than a mere suggestive coincidence. Cultural identity and maternity—femininity in its generative forces—are dominant motifs in this text which treats them as deeply felt personal experiences as well as ancestral, universal values. From the anecdotal and particularized character of the individual experience the poet widens her perspective to a more generalized view which, in spite of referring on one level to the culturally defined group, holds a universal conception of womanhood in archetypal terms.[28]

The use of Spanish is one of the differentiating factors in the poem that supports the distinctiveness of the Chicana image. Although reduced to a very few brief instances, the Spanish expressions used in the text virtually as thematic and linguistic *leit-motifs* are instrumental in the structuring and composition of the long, three-part poem; they summarize its essential meaning and pathos at strategic points, punctuating the poetic discourse with their linguistic distinctiveness. These Spanish forms identify, in contrast to the well-developed perspective of the English, the cultural values with which the poem is dealing. In spite of being written in English, the text reverberates a Chicana thematic because it precisely expresses motifs of generation and evolution— it is set at a point of change. While the mother can use both languages, with evident preference for Spanish, the daughter uses only one, her mother's language having been reduced to a mere passive function.

Much has been said about La Chingada and her historical and mythical counterparts, La Malinche and La Llorona.[29] The notion of Aztlán, with its idealized quality of a spiritual homeland, provides ample room for and a deep understanding of the inherited tradition of feminine figures which represent procreation within a world of mixed ethnic and cultural backgrounds. The conflict of identity found in most Chicano poets is achieved here in its utmost significance, with women acting naturally as the main factors in the determination of Chicano and Chicana ancestral and future values. In opposition to all the theories and manifestations of a *machista* predominance in Hispanic culture, the powerful, if in many ways subdued presence of woman as mother comes forward in dramatic and almost sacred terms.

It is quite appropriate to remember here a Latin American woman whose work as poet underscored the fundamental pre-eminence of motherhood at a moment when feminism was gathering force in the Hispanic world. Gabriela Mistral, whose lack of children of her own led her to talk about "spiritual motherhood" as a quality pertaining to every woman, voiced her conviction about the pivotal role of woman in society in terms that surpass the mere political issue of equality. In the prologue to her *Lecturas para mujeres* she wrote for Mexican women:

> Para mí la forma del patriotismo femenino es la maternidad perfecta...El patriotismo femenino es más sentimental que intelectual, y está formado, antes que de las descripciones de batallas y los relatos heroicos, de las costumbres, que la mujer crea y dirige en cierta forma; de la emoción del paisaje nativo, cuya visión afable o recia, ha ido cuajando en su alma la suavidad o la fortaleza.[30]

For her the concept of homeland was strongly related to mother-hood and to women's ability to keep alive a sense of tradition through family life and other creative activities sustained basically by a maternal love for all creatures. Womanhood appears not only as distinctly human, but also and primarily as opposed to manhood and its inherent defects, which are suggested in the reference to history being a series of battles and heroic feats.

The world of both writers, Mistral and Villanueva, seems painfully hurt by the presence of man, the lover and sire. In Mistral's works the masculine figure is barely seen as the anguished memory of someone who has abandoned the loving woman; when considered in more general terms men are presented with negative characterizations. Only infants and women partake of a true loving relationship—that of the mother and child. For Villanueva there is a concrete presence of man characterized by the violent reduction of love to rape. Like Gabriela Mistral, she alludes to man in general terms as a senseless destroyer of nature, as one opposed to the life-giving forces of woman and Earth:

> ...just
> the sight of a
> comparatively wild thing
> drives them to kill...

Woman, on the contrary, is consecrated to life and life-giving activities—the main relationship between woman and other creatures is again defined in terms of motherly love. In direct relationship to the above is the view of nature as basically pure (the feminine principle), as opposed to, or better yet, endangered by the forces of progress (the masculine will) that are an evident deformity of the essential materialism to which only women and children are really faithful. This materialism of nature, the authentic one, has little to do with the desire for possession of things characteristic of contemporary materialistic society. It has to do instead with existence, with life that is sustained by woman's procreative and nurturing capacities.

Although Villanueva's poem does not achieve the materialistic qualities of Mistral's, it is evident that among her inspirational motives the material aspect of being is still the strongest conviction. But while Mistral insisted on directly touching material things and on a concrete life among concrete things, Alma Villanueva prefers a more intellectualized approach, a direct result of a culturally different upbringing. Thus, her poetic images are less direct and seem more removed from concrete reality than those of Gabriela Mistral and other Latin American writers who are inspired by an Americanism as engaged with the question of identity as Villanueva's Chicanismo.

Even though Villanueva uses everyday situations in order to dramatize her subject, the overpowering presence in her work of poetic images with cultural and literary overtones that are far removed from popular lore demands a reading that supersedes the anecdotal and sustains meaning and aesthetic effect in abstract, intellectualized notions. The conceptual backbone of the poem sustains the obvious intent to formulate a message from the vantage point of feminist rebellion. These aspects are in consonance with a general tone of ideological commitment found in many examples of Chicana poetry, whose shortcomings can be compared with those of other poets who sustain an activist view of art and poetry.

The intellectual aura that pervades this poem could be considered as a value as much as a defect. The decision depends on the reader. For her part, the author seems to favor raw emotions and a near-to-life realism and probably was unaware of the intellectual implications that diminish the intended poetic effectiveness of her effort. The epigraphs, for instance, rather than helping in the reading of the poem obstruct it by overemphasizing the message. The texts by Octavio Paz and Adrienne Rich would have been more unobtrusive and effective if they had been put among the notes which, after all, are there as a secondary text to help the not always well-informed reader. Epigraphic citations should be less straightforward, more provocative in a suggestive sense, instead of summarizing the poem they precede. The latter type of epigraph implies a certain incomprehensibility of the poem and a need for an authorial exegesis. A poem is a work of art and deserves to be treated as such, allowing for its own text to develop a signification.

On a different order of stylistics is the metric mode of the composition. The almost invariable use of run-on verse creates lines with very harsh and awkward endings. The poem, then, develops a long sharp edge that, even as it reproduces the cutting pain of a razor blade or the stabbing thrust of violent rape at the rhythmic level, also makes it difficult to follow the rhythmic design and to read the lines as metric unities. Consequently, *La Chingada* is a text that demands from its readers a particularly well-educated poetic ear and great respect for a poetic transcription that has to be experienced without falling into automation. Alma Villanueva is as far as a poet can be from a popular-directed poetry of common language.

Even the sparse use of Spanish could be seen as another manifestation of the poem's intellectual penchant. If on the one hand it brings suggestions of a culturally based experience, as it certainly does, particularly in reference to the mother figure, on the other it can be seen as a well-versed reference to a learned value from a different culture. This type of cultural learning is fully active in the text in other very specific allusions that require a cultivated intellect in order to be decoded properly. Both readings are possible, and with them are defined two possible perspectives that the writer must have had in mind when she was working on the poem—the perspective of those Chicano readers who, like herself, are virtually native speakers of English and who know in a mostly passive way the language of their ancestors, and the perspective of her fellow Americans who are exclusively speakers of English. From each perspective the poem will be seen in a different, if not necessarily discrepant way. It seems as though Villanueva was aiming primarily at the second group, and only her mother's translation brings into consideration the less culturally adapted Chicanos.

Where the poem appears most intellectualized is in some of the images. As mentioned before, the composition combines a set of concrete, everyday images (crossing a street or walking on the beach, for instance) with images of a more abstract or symbolic character, such as the ones found at the end of Part One:

> My womb is pierced by rockets,
> space probes, trying to pierce
> the mystery of existence, trying
> to colonize the planet Venus, hotter
> than (supposedly) hell: you say,
> Venus will melt tin or lead: I say,
> my womb will melt any alien
> form of life. Venus is safe from you
> for now (out of the shell she rises for
> another day of
> love.)

Both sets of images—those taken from everyday, common experience and the symbolic ones—belong to the structural design of the poem and as such they are developed or repeated throughout the work. This characteristic, together with the division of the poem into three parts and the other aspects already mentioned, reveals its highly ambitious structure and well-developed composition. Artistic awareness and technical deftness are hallmarks of Alma Villanueva's writing.

Other aspects of the poem, like the stark opposition between man and woman, modern society and nature, highlight the categorical structure of the poet's world view. The tendency of the text is precisely to suggest opposing forces and to draw images that can be interpreted in that flash of recognition that makes good poetry such an extraordinary intellectual and emotional experience. This is the case, for instance, with the intertwinement of the two sets of images that bring together concrete reality and fantastic figuration. It is at the end of the poem that the method offers its best results. And it is only natural that this be the case, because the well-structured development of the poem demanded a movement toward its closure. The argument is simple, topical, and highly representative of an attitude which, although referring here to Chicana women, encompasses a wider, more universal feminist view. La Chingada ceases to be exclusively Mexican to become as universal in its symbolic meaning as the Venus who emerges from the sea not as a woman, but as the utmost form of the feminine principle—the earth, the ancient and loving Tellus Mater.

The mixing of different elements from different social traditions—culturally different insofar as they are social—produces a work of art which has much of Chicano uniqueness yet does not remain enclosed within the exclusive borders of Aztlán, but instead becomes part of a wider human group. Alma Villanueva's *La Chingada* does not deny its ethnic roots, but it also does not protect them from other peoples—it adds them to the common ground of humanity. If cultural identity has been dealt with previously by other poets, another form of identity—that of woman—makes it necessary to continue to write with a sense of commitment and social duty. This is why women's writing appears to be much more tense and dramatic than men's. Alma Villanueva, like Carmen Tafolla, is writing from a more combative position, from an attitude not only of commitment to social and political issues, but with a sense of duty that leads to active participation.

Carmen Tafolla

While Alma Villanueva attempts to create a system of symbols that will embody in an aesthetic and mythic discourse her clearly intellectual conception of womanhood, Carmen Tafolla follows a more realistic method by which her discourse becomes not so much an aesthetic artifact as the script for several feminine voices from different corners of Aztlán. Hers is again the poetry of popular background, the mostly direct dramatic monologue of very concrete people selected for their social representativeness. Tafolla's professional interest in social research and educational television are definitely at the base of her chosen poetic point of view.

Variety is, then, what calls one's attention in Tafolla's *La Isabela de Guadalupe y otras chucas*. Variety of voices, as indicated by the title, but also variety of themes, styles, and languages. The most significant aspect of this plurality of elements is their having been collected and organized into one book, which stresses their interrelationship. Each section of the book has for its title a verse from one of the poems included in it. The first section includes only one poem; it establishes the feminist and Chicana perspective of the book as it deals with the topic of La Chingada and the related motives of love and universal racial prejudice. A second section, centered in the Chicano past, contains several Chicano poetic motifs related to family and to cultural identity. Love, and its counterpart solitude, is the central theme of the third part, while the title of the next one—"...no me pueden chingar..."—indicates another aspect of love: sexuality and its meanings for Chicano women. A final section on the city of San Antonio treats Chicano barrio life in more general terms, relating Chicana experience to the common experience of the group.

This cursory view of the book's organization gives some sense of unity to an otherwise rambling grouping of poems. It is a prerogative of the poet to write as many poems as she wants on as many subjects as she cares about, but since it has become a custom to conceive books of poetry as coherent collections of tightly woven series of compositions, the writer has to exert her selective talent. Carmen Tafolla has not done this. She tries to have it both ways—keeping on the one hand her freedom to include all of her poems in the same collection, and on the other hand composing an organized and unitary book. While she manages to produce a rich variety of poems, the organization falters for lack of unity. The table of contents reads like a listing of well-known thematic concerns of Chicana poetry, producing, consequently, the sensation of *déjà vu*, not at all lacking in the emotional pleasures of recognition, but still a repetitive and too well known experience. There is a need in Tafolla's collection for a stricter sense of self-criticism and for more freedom from established views in Chicano poetry.

Unlike the rest of the poets included in this edition, Carmen Tafolla does not limit her poetic persona to only one Chicano speaker, as indicated before by the reference to the many voices in her poetry. Her poems offer a virtual gallery of characters, with their individual attitudes and tones. Only Leroy Quintana has tried to reproduce more than one voice from the people; El Huitlacoche draws his poetic strength from the fact that he is able to fully develop one particular speaker. Alma Villanueva and Alfonso Rodríguez, on the other hand, make little effort to characterize their poetic personae as someone other than the traditional lyrical first person of no particular fictional value. To each poet his or her own preference; the objectives are not the same, the results are also different.

For Tafolla the objective is almost anthropological in its intent to offer a realistic portrait of the Chicano people. She has a sincere interest in people as individuals and is able to see their actions and hear their words with particular accuracy. Her sense of drama and action, probably enhanced by her practice as a script writer, is quite evident and gives her poetry an anecdotal turn that is very effective in the reproduction of a popular, everyday world. As if she were holding the microphone of her tape recorder to the mouths of her informants, the poet transcribes their speech in naturally flowing verses that are generally well adapted to the voices of her subjects. These are mainly Chicana women of various ages and from different social backgrounds who represent Chicana feminine perspectives and concerns. Each one has her own language and theme. Not all of these characters sound equally convincing nor do all of them voice equally effective poems. The principal reason for this discrepancy is to be found in Tafolla's strategies of English/ Spanish usage.

Bilingualism can take different manifestations depending on the individual speakers and their preferences and circumstances. Perhaps ideally a bilingual speaker should be as proficient in one language as in the other and consequently should be able to use one or the other without losing expressive and communicative capacities in either. Still, the most common case of bilingualism among Hispanics in the United States entails using both lan- guages in a mixture regulated by a code-switching system whose rules are still to be determined. Quite aware of these linguistic peculiarities of her community of Aztlán, Carmen Tafolla as a writer uses at least three language registers, perhaps four, depending on the persona adopted as the speaker of the poem. This selectiveness is closely related to her Chicano world view and deserves further analysis and study in order to determine the cultural mechanics of its functioning.

English in its more formal poetic aspects is the register used on very few occasions. The level of proficiency is excellent and there can be no doubt about the author being a native or near-native speaker of English who has received most of her education in that language. Further proof of her proficiency in English is given by the next register—colloquial English. Colloquialisms are of fundamental importance in Tafolla's poetic language. Her technique of varying voices is very much supported by the oral aspect of language, for the several personae she chooses are dramatically characterized as true speakers talking in a concrete situation to a listener who in many cases is another person, not the reader. This colloquial English is affected by Chicano linguistic characteristics, while another linguistic register that emerges is colloquial Chicano Spanish influenced by English. Most of Tafolla's poems are written in these two forms of colloquial bilingualism that reproduce common speaking habits among Chicanos. The quality of this type of poem is a good indication of the writer's command of Chicano language both as an everyday form of communication and as a means for poetic expression. Probably her best compositions belong to this group.

Most of Tafolla's love poems belong to a different register. Curiously enough, the language in this case is formal Spanish. What is surprising in these compositions is the fact that they are written in the weakest and most formulaic of her linguistic registers. None of the poems in Spanish reaches the level of literary quality of the rest. It would appear that the level of the poet's proficiency in Spanish does not include literary sophistication. Still, her Spanish poems are worthy of inclusion in the book because of their cultural interest—they represent the true expression of a particular speaker who, for reasons that will be necessary to analyze, when talking to her lover feels the need to do it in Spanish. One wonders how much "machismo al revés" is inadvertently voiced here.

The masculine figure is very present in Tafolla's work, contrary to what happens in Villanueva's poem. Comparing both

writers' treatment of love would be an excellent exercise in
understanding the tensions present in the Chicana's fight for an
identity as woman within her own world of Aztlán. A quick review
of the articles on Chicana poetry shows an overwhelming primacy
of the problems related to the search for a Chicana identity in
ethno-cultural and feminist terms.[31] To avoid repeating concepts
already discussed by critics and poets, it will be better to focus on
the subject of man/woman relationships, a motif of utmost
interest to the Chicana poets who are still trying to establish their
own independence and identity as women.

Little can be said about love in relation to the works of the male
poets here presented. In Rodríguez' psalms there are only vague
indications of filial love and a sense of matrimonial commitment
to a life of sacrifice and dedication to family and group survival.
All of this is only implied in the dedication of the book to the poet's
parents; nothing of this sort is to be found affecting the symbolic
view of the work. Love as an emotional relationship between man
and woman is practically absent in Quintana's poems; only sex as
an external manifestation appears vaguely. A funny situation
involving a marital quarrel is alluded to in one poem where the
theme is the blind forces that bind lovers together. A rather ironic
reference to interracial love touches lightly on the warm feeling of
a long-lost juvenile affair. In El Huitlacoche sex is an important
measure of man's love life, and although there are examples of
caring feelings for woman and family in his poetry, the poet
stresses a machista attitude toward sexual relationships.

To the self-centered sexual interest manifest in the works of the
male poets, and to the absence of love as a significant motive in
many of their poems, Alma Villanueva adds her claim for woman's
freedom from man's sexual attack. The picture is far from
comforting and bespeaks a profound rift in the emotional state of
la chicanada. Even Carmen Tafolla, who appears to oppose this
picture with her strong feelings of companionship and a traditional feminine view of love as an act of giving, also represents a
problematic situation. Man is still an almost invisible object of
desire, as in the poem "Quisiera," which ends with a repeated
sentence that summarizes woman's predicament:

> Pero las estrellas adoloridas y la pobre luna
>   tendrán que esperar.
> La noche sola y la brisa loca
>   tendrán que esperar.

El triste sol y la mañana enamorada
            tendrán que esperar.
Y mis mil besos de amor para ti
            ¡tendrán que esperar!

Man becomes less important than love itself, a mere object, perhaps because of his own lack of commitment to a relationship with woman:

Te beso
    y te sigo besando
    siglo tras siglo
        sin poder jamás
            sentirte otra
                cosa que
                    el puro
                        amor.

The complete fourth section of the book offers a view of woman in strong opposition to man, echoing the feeling of superiority sensed in Mistral and Villanueva. The poem on La Malinche poses the main attitude of feminine complaint and rebellion against male predominance. "La Isabela de Guadalupe y el apache Mío Cid," the first poem of the book, also deals with the subject of La Chingada and represents Chicana women as slaves of men:

En España, gitana
En México, criada
Y hasta entre Aztecas,
yo no fui Azteca, sino obrera,
cara triste,
y calma.

The difference between man and woman, the Spaniard and the Indian, the conqueror and the conquered is also striking:

I, que me gusta andar descalza,
y tú, bordado en hilos de oro,
    How can we ever make love?

"How can we ever make love?" is a question repeated several times in the poem, and it can be asked only by someone who wants love but understands the impossibility of getting it under the circumstances. The end of the poem, with the word "amamos" (in Spanish!) after a series of verses that gradually move from English to Spanish, insists on love's power as a supreme force that surpasses the limited relationship between man and woman. It talks about universal love. The caring and loving expressed by Tafolla as well as by Villanueva's strongest defense of femininity conclude in an optimistic faith in love, the natural cosmic force which, through woman's capacity for accepting and assuming it, sustains the essence of human life and continuity. Among the men only Alfonso Rodríguez approaches a similar view of transcendental realism.

Conclusion

No introduction to these five poets of Aztlán could have paid attention to all the critical matters raised by their very different voices. Each of them requires a specific approach; all of them deserve a careful reading and interpretation free of the constraints of an extremely self-conscious perspective that gives merit mostly to ethnic qualities and pays less attention to literary values.[32] I have tried to point to some characteristics I believe may lead to further literary studies that will make possible a reading not necessarily influenced by mostly ethnographic and sociological interests. The texts here presented, like all literary texts, are to be read not only as examples of Chicano literature—which they certainly are—but also, and primarily, as authentically artistic achievements of individuals living in a particular place at a given time in history.

Historical and sociological circumstances are in no way factors adverse to artistic greatness and its universal recognition. No work of art has ever been achieved in isolation from the immediate circumstances, and many a great one has been definitely aimed at dealing with these circumstances for very practical purposes. Of the five poets included in this collection none can be accused of— or praised for—having evaded the specific Chicano circumstances, a fact that at this point weighs little in favor of or against their appreciation. Even if our critical sense allowed us to see in their texts only the most external aspects of style, we would still be aware of their particular cultural and historical antecedents; their poetry is so well ingrained in two literary traditions—those of Latin America and the United States—that their voices have the familiar tones of many contemporary non-Chicano authors.

A danger to which these five poets are exposed—as are all those who define their art in terms of its ethnic distinctiveness—is to be reduced by public and critics alike to the limiting circles of minority literature in the United States and to accept this status as a definitive fact. Although very few writers of any nation achieve the aim of being read by a world-wide public, some have more possibilities than others of achieving it because of extraliterary factors such as commercial policies governing the publishing, release, and distribution of literary works. Chicano writers, as for many years was the case of Latin American writers, are being intrinsically affected by these apparently external factors whose effects on the development of a literature are much more important than what critics normally like to think. If on the one hand they influence the reading public, on the other they also exert no little pressure on the writers themselves, who cannot work in a vacuum, disregarding the realities of their profession.

It seems obvious, then, that Chicano writers, critics, and publishers have to fight, without abandoning their own identities as Chicanos, for a wider arena of action that should include, at least, the reading public of both Americas. But no matter how much effort is made in these practical matters of literary promotion, no new ground will be won for Chicano literature if the poets do not do their part—write well. Equally responsible are the critics, who have to value writers on purely artistic—that is to say, professional—grounds rather than on sentimentally and ideologically prejudiced notions of ethnic identification and cultural self-subserviency. Only when writers and critics act with a true sense of literary responsibility that first and foremost is based on the will and dedication to be proficient in their trade does literature become of interest and value for all.

UNIVERSITY OF WISCONSIN-MILWAUKEE

Notes

1. Of the different translations given to the Aztec term Aztlán, I have taken one that I particularly like for its poetic connotations. Francisco J. Santamaría in the article on "Azteca" in *Diccionario de mejicanismos* (México: Porrua, 1959) translates Aztlán as "Lugar de Garzas." This is similar to the "Crane People" given by Ed Ludwig in the introduction to *The Chicanos: Mexican American Voices* (Baltimore: Penguin Books, 1971), p. 5. Ludwig also gives as a translation "The Place of Reeds," which I have adopted for my title. The term "voices" in this title also requires a brief commentary. In spite of the fact that there are several anthologies using the same term to refer to Chicano writers, I have decided to use it

because it applies exactly to my view of the poetry of these authors as the verbal expression of different Chicano literary personae talking, using their own voices.
   2. Despite certain limitations and lacunae, there exist significant bibliographic resources for both Chicano literature and Chicano literary criticism. A logical starting place for identifying and utilizing these resources is Roberto G. Trujillo, "Bibliography," in *A Decade of Chicano Literature (1970-1979): Critical Essays and Bibliography*, eds. Luis Leal, Fernando de Necochea, Francisco Lomelí, and Roberto G. Trujillo (Santa Barbara, CA: Editorial La Causa, 1982), 95-106. Trujillo's review identifies and analyzes the positive features and drawbacks of a number of bibliographic resources for Chicano literary criticism and/or Chicano literature itself, including: Guillermo Rojas, "Towards a Chicano/Raza Bibliography: Drama, Prose, Poetry," *El Grito*, 7, 2 (Dec., 1973); Francisco Lomelí and Donaldo W. Urioste, *Chicano Perspectives in Literature: A Critical and Annotated Bibliography* (Albuquerque: Pajarito Publications, 1976); Charles M. Tatum, *A Selected and Annotated Bibliography of Chicano Studies*, 2nd ed. (Lincoln, Nebraska: Univ. of Nebraska, Society of Spanish and Spanish-American Studies, 1979); Ernestina N. Eger, "A Selected Bibliography of Chicano Criticism," in *The Identification and Analysis of Chicano Literature*, ed. Francisco Jiménez (New York: Bilingual Press/Editorial Bilingüe, 1979), 389-403; the *Chicano Periodical Index* (Boston: G.K. Hall, 1981); and Ernestina N. Eger, *A Bibliography of Criticism of Contemporary Chicano Literature* (Berkeley: Univ. of California Chicano Studies Library, 1982). For Chicano literary criticism the most comprehensive and up-to-date source is the last citation, Eger's bibliography, which identifies 2,181 items published in books, journals, magazines, newspapers, videotapes, theses, dissertations, conference papers, reprints, excerpts, unpublished sources, and works in progress. An excellent starting place for identifying the body of Chicano creative literature is the book in which Trujillo's article appears, *A Decade of Chicano Literature (1970-1979)*, which compiles a bibliography of over 325 works categorized into the following areas: poetry, novels, short fiction, theater, literary criticism, literatura chicanesca, oral tradition in print, anthologies, Chicano literary periodicals, unpublished dissertations, and bibliographies. I take this opportunity to supplement the resources analyzed in Trujillo's article with some additional titles. (1) Julio A. Martínez, *Chicano Scholars and Writers: A Bio-Bibliographical Directory* (Metuchen, N.J.: Scarecrow Press, 1979). Despite being somewhat out of date and despite certain inaccuracies and omissions, this work remains a useful reference tool because, fashioned like an individual's curriculum vitae, it contains not only references to works but other significant biographical data. (2) Elizabeth Ordóñez, "Chicana Literature and Related Sources: A Selected and Annotated Bibliography," *The Bilingual Review/La Revista Bilingüe*, Vol. VII, No. 2 (May-August, 1980), 143-164, an annotated, critical bibliography of 198 titles categorized into bibliographies, general works (Chicana feminism, folklore, history), anthologies, poetry, fiction, drama, general literary criticism, plastic arts, film, works by men with significant women figures or themes, related sources, and useful addresses (periodicals, newsletters, book distributors). (3) Enid Zimmerman, "An Annotated Bibliography of Chicano Literature: Novels, Short Fiction, Poetry, and Drama, 1970-1980," *The Bilingual Review/La Revista Bilingüe*, Vol. IX, No. 3 (Sept.-Dec. 1982), a very thorough, critical bibliography of Chicano literature. (4) Jorge A. Huerta, *Chicano Theatre: Themes and Forms* (Ypsilanti, MI: Bilingual

Press, 1982), the bibliography for which contains 572 citations on Chicano and Mexican theater.

3. It is necessary to observe that the preference for poetry among Chicanos should also be interpreted as the consequence of other less directly literary factors. Joel Hancock points to an important sociological datum when he writes that "poetry unquestionably enjoys the greatest popularity and circulation" and explains that "this is due in part to the facilities for publication." "The Emergence of Chicano Poetry: A Survey of Sources, Themes, and Techniques," *Arizona Quarterly*, 21, 1 (1973), 58.

4. See note 2 above. This text is indispensable for the student of Chicano literature. It not only contains a very helpful bibliography, but it addresses the central points related to the criticism of literature as applied to the particular case of Chicano letters.

5. Carlota Cárdenas de Dwyer, "Chicano Poetry," *Literary Criterion*, 12, 1 (1975), 23-35. Felipe de Ortego sustains the view that Chicano literature forms part of the American experience. See his preface to *We Are Chicanos* (New York: Washington Square Press, 1973), pp. XII-XVI, and "An Introduction to Chicano Poetry," in Joseph Sommers and Tomás Ybarra-Frausto, eds., *Modern Chicano Writers* (Englewood Cliffs, NJ: Prentice-Hall, 1979), pp. 108-116.

6. Rolando Hinojosa, "Mexican-American Literature: Toward an Identification," in *The Identification and Analysis of Chicano Literature*, pp. 7-18.

7. For a discussion of the relationship between everyday, communal Chicano language and the artistic elaboration in Chicano literature which springs from the former but is distinct from it, see: Gary D. Keller, "The Literary Strategems Available to the Bilingual Chicano Writer," in *The Identification and Analysis of Chicano Literature*, 263-316; John M. Lipski, "Spanish-English Language Switching in Speech and Literature: Theories and Models," *The Bilingual Review/La Revista Bilingüe*, Vol. IX, No. 3 (Sept.-Dec. 1982), 191-212; Gary D. Keller, "Toward a Stylistic Analysis of Bilingual Texts: From Ernest Hemingway to Contemporary Boricua and Chicano Literature," in *The Analysis of Hispanic Texts: Current Trends in Methodology*, ed. Mary Ann Beck, Lisa E. Davis, José Hernández, Gary D. Keller and Isabel C. Tarán (New York: Bilingual Press, 1976), 130-149. An earlier view developed by scholars such as Guadalupe Valdés and Herminio Ríos, which is now superseded but which occasionally still finds expression, saw a much closer relationship between artistic Chicano usage and daily Chicano usage in society than what obtains as a result of close scholarly scrutiny. See: Guadalupe Valdés-Fallis, "The Sociolinguistics of Chicano Literature: Towards an Analysis of the Role and Function of Language Alternation in Contemporary Bilingual Poetry," *Point of Contact/Punto de contacto*, I, 4 (1977), 30-39; Guadalupe Valdés-Fallis, "Code-Switching in Bilingual Chicano Poetry," *Hispania*, 59 (1976), 877-886; Herminio Ríos, "Introduction," *El Grito*, Book 3, Year VII (1974), p. 7; Carlota Cárdenas de Dwyer, "Poetry," in *A Decade of Chicano Literature (1970-1979): Critical Essays and Bibliography* (Santa Barbara, CA: Editorial La Causa, 1982), 19-28.

8. For Sergio D. Elizondo, Chicano literature has developed a "fundamentally realistic" character due to the writer's "intentional literary commitment." He explains that "reality in Chicano literature is one factor that, by definition, emerges from the most vital concerns of the Chicano people; it is clear that the literary

themes derive from the everyday reality of the Chicano." "Myth and Reality in Chicano Literature," *Latin American Literary Review*, V, 10 (1977), 23.

9. Luis Leal, "The Problem of Identifying Chicano Literature," in *The Identification and Analysis of Chicano Literature*, pp. 2-5.

10. Salvador Rodríguez del Pino talks about the "Poetas de la nueva trayectoria" as those who "tratan de alcanzar universalidad sin dejar de pisar sus raíces." "La poesía chicana: Una nueva trayectoria," in *The Identification and Analysis of Chicano Literature*, p. 79. The problem of universality will continue to define much of Chicano literary thought in future years. The matter has already been brought to light by the critics; see, for instance, Sylvia Gonzales, "National Character vs. Universality in Chicano Poetry," in *The Chicano Literary World 1974*, edited by Felipe Ortego and David Conde (Las Vegas, NM: New Mexico Highlands University, 1975), pp. 13-28; and *De Colores*, I, 4 (1975), pp. 10-21.

11. Carmen Salazar Parr comments that, in general, "Chicano critics have been polarized into two groups: those who see Chicano literature as reflecting the socio-historical and cultural reality of the Chicano and those who defend it in terms of universal, transcendental values." "Current Trends in Chicano Literary Criticism," in *The Identification and Analysis of Chicano Literature*, p. 134. An important article that describes the existing critical approaches and presents a model for future critical studies is Joseph Sommers, "Critical Approaches to Chicano Literature," in *The Identification and Analysis of Chicano Literature*, pp. 143-152; also in *Modern Chicano Writers*, pp. 31-40. Another version of the same article appeared in *The New Scholar*, 6 (1977), pp. 51-80, with the title: "From the Critical Premise to the Product: Critical Modes and Their Applications to a Chicano Literary Text."

12. See Adolfo Ortega, "Of Social Politics and Poetry: A Chicano Perspective," *Latin American Literary Review*, 5, 10 (1977), 32-41; and Tomás Ybarra-Frausto, "The Chicano Movement and the Emergence of a Chicano Poetic Consciousness," *New Scholar*, 6, (1977), 81-109.

13. It seems natural for critics of Chicano literature to be unable to avoid adopting a culturalist point of view, particularly when they are faced with the coincidence of the social and literary awakenings of the group. If they want to address their fellow Chicanos they insist on their identity as culturally determined individuals; if they are to address the rest of the American people, they feel compelled to be as informative as possible with respect to the distinctively Chicano experience and world view. The several anthologies prepared for the non-Chicano public are good examples of this fact. See, for instance, one of the most representative of this critical attitude: *Literatura Chicana: Texto y Contexto/ Chicano Literature: Text and Context*, edited by Antonia Castañeda Shular, Tomás Ybarra-Frausto and Joseph Sommers (Englewood Cliffs, NJ: Prentice Hall, 1972).

14. Volumes I and II; edited by Gary D. Keller and Francisco Jiménez (Ypsilanti, MI: Bilingual Press/Editorial Bilingüe, 1980 and 1982).

15. Sergio D. Elizondo, "Myth and Reality in Chicano Literature," *Latin American Literary Review*, V. 10 (1977), 23-31.

16. The fact that the "Spiritual Plan of Aztlán" was the work of a political activist-poet like "Corky" Gonzales and also the invention of another poet, Alurista, is something that has to be taken into consideration when dealing with the function of poetry in the formulation of a Chicano identity. In "Alurista, poeta-antropólogo, and the Recuperation of the Chicano Identity," Gary D. Keller

comments that, as observed by Luis Leal, "Alurista was perhaps the first who at the level of literature and formal ideology (in contrast to popular usages, where earlier examples can be attested to) established—in 1968-69—the concept of a Chicano Aztlán: a symbol—cultural, political, geographic, and above all, mythic—of the aspirations of la Raza." In Alurista, *Return: Poems Collected and New* (Ypsilanti, MI: Bilingual Press/Editorial Bilingüe, 1982), p. xv.

17. See Elizabeth J. Ordóñez, "Chicana Literature and Related Sources: A Selected and Annotated Bibliography," *The Bilingual Review/La Revista Bilingüe*, VII, 2 (1980), 143-164.

18. In their introduction to *Modern Chicano Writers* (p. 1), Sommers and Ybarra-Frausto point to the relationship between the socio-cultural circumstances and the language of Chicano literature: "Our fundamental assumption in making this collection is that Chicano literature is a form of cultural expression by a people who have survived and grown through responding to conditions of domination. The literary consequences of these conditions have been crucial. One is the lack of access to education and a resulting cultural emphasis on oral expression and transmission rather than print. A second is the conception of literature as a local or regional phenomenon. Yet another consequence lies in the series of issues associated with language." These issues refer mostly to bilingualism as a socio-cultural characteristic observed by most critics in the linguistic code-switching of many Chicano poems; for Bruce-Novoa, "Chicanos do not function as constantly choice-making speakers; their language is a blend, a synthesis of the two into a third. Thus they are interlingual, not bilingual. The codes are not separate, but intrinsically fused." *Chicano Authors: Inquiry by Interview* (Austin and London: University of Texas Press, 1980), p. 29.

19. See the references in note 7, above.

20. Although critics have commented on the "stylistic multilingualism" of Alurista, as Gary D. Keller does in "Alurista, poeta-antropólogo . . . ", pp. xxxix ff., it is important to observe that bilingualism is a characteristic of everyday language and its use as poetic language is also dictated by a natural need to write in the language of habitual communication.

21. The image of the mirror appears in the title of one of the first anthologies of Chicano literature, *El espejo/The Mirror*, edited by Octavio Ignacio Romano-V (Berkeley, CA: Quinto Sol Publications, 1969); it is obvious that in this case it is used to signify the reflective character of Chicano literary creation. The same image is also used by Rafael Jesús González in "Chicano Poetry: Smoking Mirror," *New Scholar*, 6, (1977), pp. 127-138.

22. There is an evident influence of leftist ideologies in the literary manifestations of the Chicano, particularly in the early days of social consciousness-raising. In 1972 Fernando Alegría wrote: "Por el momento no puedo concebir la literatura chicana sino como una expresión directa de un movimiento social que empieza con signos de rebelión masiva contra el *establishment* capitalista norteamericano, y en los últimos diez años, va transformándose en una revolución ideológicamente identificada con el Tercer Mundo." *Hispamérica*, 2 (1972), p. 37. Arturo Pérez maintains the same attitude a few years later in "Poesía Chicana," *Cuadernos Hispanoamericanos*, 325 (1977), pp. 123-131. The similarities between the Chicano and Third World political and social conditions are not negligible and pose another analytic task for the critic who wishes to see Chicano literature included among the rest of Latin American national literatures.

23. See the biographical notes on each poet. The five authors included in this edition have in common a similar biographical experience—they have reached high positions among intellectual groups, having been born to economically disadvantaged families.

24. See above, note 10. As Carmen Salazar Parr has pointed out in "Current Trends in Chicano Literary Criticism," critics have been divided into two main groups, depending on their preference for a culturalist or a universalist interpretation of Chicano literature. She gives the names of Guadalupe Valdés, Sylvia Gonzales, and Juan Bruce-Novoa as the most representative of the universalist view. As other critics follow their example, the universal values of Chicano poetry will become more evident and writers themselves will feel encouraged to experiment with new themes and new approaches in the interpretation of their personal experiences of the world.

25. The influence of Ernesto Cardenal and his religious and political ideas is evident in Rodríguez' work. The title of his collection recalls to a certain extent Cardenal's *Salmos* (Buenos Aires: Carlos Lohlé, 1969), while the theological views on social change follow very closely Cardenal's concept of the Kingdom of God on Earth, developed from a post-conciliar view of social justice in the Third World. See: Fernando Jorge Flores, "Comunismo o reino de Dios: una aproximación a la experiencia religiosa de Ernesto Cardenal," in *Ernesto Cardenal, poeta de la liberación latinoamericana*, edited by Elisa Calabrese (Buenos Aires: Fernando García Cambeiro, 1975), pp. 159-190. For an introduction to Latin American theological concerns during the last decades, see: José Miguel Bonino, *Doing Theology in a Revolutionary Situation* (Philadelphia: Fortress Press, 1975).

26. Larry M. Grimes, *El tabú lingüístico en México: El lenguaje erótico de los mexicanos* (New York: Bilingual Press/Editorial Bilingüe, 1978).

27. There already are several articles devoted to the poetry of Alma Villanueva: Alejandro Morales, "Terra Mater and the Emergence of Myth in *Poems* by Alma Villanueva," *The Bilingual Review/La Revista Bilingüe*, 7, 2 (1980), pp. 123-142; Elizabeth Ordóñez, "Alma Villanueva," *Chicano Literature*, ed. Julio Martínez and Francisco Lomelí (Westport, CT: Greenwood Press, 1984). Ordóñez has also written a review of Villanueva's book of poems *Bloodroot* in *Revista Chicano-Riqueña*, 6, 4 (1978).

28. Alejandro Morales, "Terra Mater and the Emergence of Myth in *Poems* by A.V.," studies the archetype in Villanueva's poetry; see note 27.

29. An idea of the number of texts related to La Malinche, La Llorona, and La Chingada can be obtained in Elizabeth Ordóñez, "Chicana Literature and Related Sources: A Selected and Annotated Bibliography" (see note 2).

30. México: Secretaría de Educación, 1923, p. 10.

31. See Elizabeth Ordóñez' bibliography on Chicana literature.

32. Ricardo Valdés, "Defining Chicano Literature, or the Perimeters of Literary Space," *Latin American Literary Review*, 5, 10 (1977), pp. 16-22, suggests the need to use an eclectic method to critically approach Chicano literature; each work deserves its own critical point of view, the one that is most suitable to the work's characteristics.

Salmos para migrantes

Alfonso Rodríguez

Alfonso Rodríguez was born in the state of Coahuila, México, in 1943. At the age of eleven he moved to Texas with his family. He graduated from Crystal City High School in 1963. For many years he and his family traveled to the Midwest as migrant workers. Rodríguez attended Southwest Texas Junior College in Uvalde where he completed his Associate of Arts Degree in 1965. Subsequently he transferred to Texas A&I University. There, he did his B.A. and M.A. degrees in the areas of Spanish, political science, and education. For several years he was involved in migrant education, and he has been a teacher at both the elementary and high school levels. At the University of Iowa he studied Spanish and Latin American literatures, obtaining his Ph.D. in 1976. He taught at Northern Illinois University for three years. He has served as chairman of the Department of Mexican-American Studies at the University of Northern Colorado. At present he is an associate professor in the new Department of Hispanic Studies at the same institution. Rodríguez is a firm believer in cultural democracy and bilingual-multicultural education.

In addition to his poetry he has written short stories and literary criticism. His work has appeared in such journals as *Cuadernos Americanos, Cuadernos Hispanoamericanos, De Colores, Bilingual Review,* and others. Rodríguez is married and has two daughters.

Publications Related to Chicano Studies

Creative Literature

"El hombre junto al río" (short story). In *Hispanics in the United States: An Anthology of Creative Literature.* Ed. Gary D. Keller and Francisco Jiménez. Ypsilanti, MI: Bilingual Press, 1980. Pp. 141-43. Also in *Mosaico de la vida: Narrativa chicana, cubana y puertorriqueña.* Ed. Francisco Jiménez. New York: Harcourt Brace Jovanovich, 1981. Pp. 132-36.

"La otra frontera" (short story). In *Hispanics in the United States: An Anthology of Creative Literature. Vol. II.* Ed. Francisco Jiménez and Gary D. Keller. Ypsilanti, MI: Bilingual Press, 1982. Pp. 3-9.

"Mañana será otro día" (short story). *Revista Río Bravo* (Laredo, Texas), Vol. II, No. 1 (Spring 1982), pp. 8, 16-18.

Research and Scholarship

"Teaching Spanish to Chicanos." *Thresholds in Secondary Education* (Northern Illinois University), Vol. II, No. 2 (Summer 1976), pp. 17-18, 32.

"Samuel Ramos: Influencia de Adler y Jung en su estudio sobre el carácter del mexicano." *Cuadernos Hispanoamericanos*, Nos. 326-27 (agosto-septiembre 1977).

"El motivo del engaño en el *Popol Vuh*." *Cuadernos Americanos*, Vol. CCXXVI, No. 5 (septiembre-octubre 1979).

"Tragic Vision in Estela Portillos's *The Day of the Swallows*." *De Colores: Journal of Chicano Expression and Thought*, Vol. 5, Nos. 1 & 2.

"Time as a Structural Device in Rivera's *...y no se lo tragó la tierra*." In *Contemporary Chicano Fiction: A Critical Survey*. Ed. Vernon Lattin. Binghamton, NY: Bilingual Press (forthcoming).

A mis padres,
que han caminado como
contemplando el rostro de la esperanza.

Para qué llamar caminos
a los surcos del azar,
todo el que camina anda
como Jesús en el mar.
　　　　—Antonio Machado

…a fin de que sepáis
el camino por donde habéis
de ir; por cuanto vosotros
no habéis pasado antes de ahora
por este camino.
　　　　—Josué 3:4

I

Hoy te acostarás
    cuando esté muy entrada
        la noche en sus asuntos.
Terminarás
    al fin,
    los trámites del día
    para empezar de nuevo
    el viaje hacia mañana.

Tu cuerpo no reposará
    pues tu alma estará llena
        de muchos pormenores,
como cojín
    cubierto de alfileres
    que punzan
    muy quedito.
Te levantarás,
    como de costumbre,
        muy de madrugada;
y atarantado de sueño
    y de cansancio
    te entregarás a Dios
    y a la jornada.

Tu corazón te avisará
    que con el tiempo
    no se juega,
y mucho menos cuando el tiempo
    está hecho de camino
    pues desde niño te enseñaron
    que caminando se viven las verdades.

Dejarás tu rincón
    íntimamente cotidiano
        como se deja a un compañero,
casi hermano,

que se nos va,
se nos acaba
y se queda en el tiempo rezagado.

Conversarás con el camino
        por tramos incansables
                y aprenderás lo que otras veces
únicamente imaginaste
                lo que jamás se aprende
                buscando entre los libros
                de los planteles de este mundo.

Tarde o temprano
        te estrecharán
                las tempestades en su vuelo;
te llamarán con su murmullo
                grandilocuente, oscuro
                en el momento que tú estimes
                más inoportuno.

Te sentirás muy aturdido
        tal vez desamparado,
                pero no arrepentido,
pues sólo Dios sabe
                desde cuándo
                tu camino y el de las tempestades
                son el mismo.

II

Mientras caminas,
entra el camino en tu corazón
abriéndose paso
como una enredadera,
y tú te llenas de mucha geografía.

La herida del tiempo
se dibuja en tu rostro
con estilo certero y penetrante,
como decreto infalible;
y la vida te va doliendo a cada paso;
luminosa en otras ocasiones,
tu mirada se tiñe de un gris despoblado
como una despedida en tarde fría
como la soledad de un puente abandonado.

¡Cuántas angustias que ya no recordabas
trae a tu pensamiento tu cansancio!

¡Cuántas jornadas envejeces
para que cambie de parecer tu letanía!

Vas aferrado al camino
abriendo caminos en el aire,
sembrando, mientras pasas, la esperanza,
regándola con gotas de tu sangre.

¿Quién sabe si algún día, con los años,
alguien recordará que por aquí pasaste?

¿Quién sabe si algún día, en el camino,
por fin florecerá lo que sembraste?

Mas el camino caminado
no será nunca caminado en vano.

III

Dejo que la mirada
se pasee por las lejanías
y te diviso a ti,
             migrante hermano;
atribulado, sin remedio,
             con tu sueño;
      allí van por el tiempo,
como gemelos adversarios
      tu sueño que no muere,
             y tú,
imagen que se pierde en el camino,
      en conflicto
como el perro y el gato,
             sin identificarse,
      pero sin separarse
             uno del otro,
como mamíferos hermanos
      como enemigos declarados.

Migrante:
tú y tu sueño son los únicos
      que van de viaje en esta noche;
y reconoces que el latido
             entre tus muros
está hecho de tiempo,
             de tiempo irreversible,
y de una historia
      que nunca se ha contado
pero que algunos han querido
             grabar en las tinieblas

Migrante:
tu corazón que late muy dolido
      en estos recorridos
es semejante a un suspiro

que pasa bambaleándose
como gigante herido,
que se desploma sobre el suelo
de tus esperanzas;
pero vuelves a la faena
que ya te sabes de memoria:
a duras penas lo levantas
y le infundes nueva vida
y sigues caminando
hacia tu tierra prometida ...

IV

Hermano pasajero:
el tiempo que vas dejando
atrás al caminar
ya no te pertence,
es sólo arena difusa
que va pasando a la memoria;
el tiempo que vas buscando
entre las rotaciones anónimas
de tu cronología,
¿quién sabe si rendirá
sus frutos esperados?
El que cuenta
es el tiempo entre tus manos,
el que se esfuma
como la edad
de grises pensamientos.
¿En qué momento pasa el instante
a ser recuerdo?
¿En qué momento
pasan tus palpitaciones
a la historia?

V

... y sigues caminando ...

Los suspiros del viento
    recorren distancias desconocidas;
la noche pierde su dominio
    y desaparece
como el instante que la justifica ...

    ... y tú caminando ...

El sol castiga la sensibilidad del rocío
    y lo condena a un destierro prolongado;
por un segundo, el mediodía
    hace una síntesis de todas las edades ...

    ... y tú caminando ...

La tarde se yergue y desplaza
    a toda criatura humana de su reino;
la claridad está contigo
    y sin embargo, inalcanzable, como un astro ...

    ... y tú caminando ...

El calor se ensancha y te hiere
    con la furia de ángel despiadado,
y te acerca al terreno
    de las más grandes inquietudes ...

    ... y tú caminando ...

El viento se encapricha
    y vuelve a vivir su mitología;
otra noche emprende sus nuevos menesteres
    y acentúa unos gestos más vagos todavía...

    ... y tú caminando ...

Algo toca un ámbito profundo,
    un sentimiento imponderable que te llama,
y tú detienes tu mirada, recapacitas,
    y encuentras el motivo de tu nueva esperanza ...

    ... y sigues caminando ...

VI

              Migrante:
el desgaste de tu barro
te pone la vista vidriosa
y tu perspectiva se reparte
por todas las edades,
en mil fragmentos,
en el sol reverberante;
              titubeas
              tropiezas
              caes
              mueres entre
              tus propios brazos
              resucitas
              luchas
              contra ti mismo
              contra los elementos
              contra oscuras justicias;
aferrado a la misma caminata.
Tu alma repite las mismas advertencias
y no registras la crónica
de tus adversidades,
siempre abrazado a tus preceptos
por esos caminos de huellas ilegibles,
siguiendo una señal que sólo tú descifras:
un trozo de dolor
que desemboca en la esperanza.

VII

Por entre lo más denso
　　de la pobreza
　　　　pasas hollando
　　　　　su sonrisa burlona.
Y ella queda dolida
　　en su orgullo
　　　　de diosa redonda
　　　　　y compleja.
Con su actitud fría,
　　consuetudinaria,
　　　　dibuja heridas
　　　　　en tu corazón.
Y salen volando a borbotones
　　mariposas desnutridas
　　　　teñidas de un color
　　　　　que tira a desamparo.
Abren senderos en la quietud cálida
　　y vuelven a esconderse
　　　　en su origen;
　　　　　mientras tú, viajero,
pasas despellejado bajo una lluvia
　　de desprecios horizontales
　　　　sin saber si el próximo paso
　　　　　será firme o será en falso.

VIII

    Migrante:
conforme a la ley de todo caminante,
    tu vida es nomás pasar,
        pasar como siempre pasas,
dejando huellas sin rostro,
    por los llanos ...
        dejando un vaho en el aire,
por los bosques ...
    dejando ruegos dispersos,
        por la faz del horizonte ...
dejando tu suerte en vilo
    por donde a nadie conoces ...
        y siempre es soñar despierto,
en silencio y dando voces,
    como las naves sin puerto ...

IX

    Migrante:
eres un poeta sin palabras;
    tu corazón comulga con la aurora
en escueta ceremonia;
    visita los vericuetos
de los ciclos solitarios;
    se entiende a la distancia
con los atardeceres soñolientos;
    siente el fluir de la esperanza
en el desierto de la nada;
    se queda, de improviso, estupefacto
en las palpitaciones
    que marcan el ritmo de la noche;
cuando sólo cuentan
    Dios, tu soledad, y la Palabra
que sólo bulle dentro de tu alma.

X

Espinas venenosas
dan en el blanco de tu centro.
El destino es el vendabal;
y tú, su pasatiempo.
La desesperación aprieta el paso
como si fuera en asunto de emergencia;

Serenidad.
Desasosiego.
Equidistantes de tu alma.

La tristeza tiene manos de seda
y la mirada que no se quiebra.

Dentro de ti retumba la Palabra;
es suprimida
sufre
sangra
presiente
muere prematuramente
y vuelve hacia la vida.

¡Cómo quisiera la aflicción
arrastrarte en el hueco de su remolino!

Mas no das a torcer
el hierro que te alienta;
una esperanza en silencio
vuelve a ti multiplicada ...

De pronto sientes un hambre
que te muerde las entrañas,
hambre de fundamentos,
de fundamentos perdurables ...

Y así, a paso lento,
vas hacia el fondo de tu herida
   porque a pesar de los pesares
      tienes un compromiso con la vida ...

XI

      Hay un instante
que se queda dando vueltas en torno a sí mismo,
como buscando algo perdido
como agitando la carga de los años;
         y luego se esfuma para siempre.
  Mientras tanto,
  tú vas pasando
      con ademanes de humana trascendencia,
      queriendo retener
      el tiempo entre tus sueños
      ansiando revivir
      ese instante que fue tuyo,
en medio del furor y el caos
de un mundo que va perdiendo ya
el juicio de su sombra.

      El camino
te va despojando gota a gota
  del fuego que fluye por tus sienes.
Tus acontecimientos están escritos
en textos de carne al rojo vivo.
      Se sufre,
      pero se aprende caminando;
      el barro
      se va desgastando como nada
      pero tu ser
      se va renovando como el agua.

En tu trayectoria incontenible
vas en pos de lo que otros menosprecian;
    no buscando las cosas
    que se divisan con los ojos,
        sino las que se contemplan con el alma,
        pues esas vivencias inefables
        llenan la mirada de esperanza.

XII

La niebla es sólo
    la respiración de la tierra
en el momento más explícito
    de la noche;
una música suave y arcaica
    por el camino del recuerdo
llega hasta ti
    desde quién sabe dónde;
la estación pasa,
    su rostro cubierto
con el velo fugitivo del tiempo;
    no ves provecho alguno en el camino;
con todo, algo sublime
    murmura muy cerca de tu alma
y desentierra melancolías olvidadas;
    precavida, retrocede
una emoción dentro de ti
    y luego vuelves
a marcar tus pasos;
    caminas pensativo
        sin palabras
        sin gesticulaciones
        sin percibir siquiera
lo que tu propio corazón
    te va diciendo;
el viento pasa
    a regañadientes, desafinado y testarudo

siguiendo siempre su costumbre;
la noche lleva una fusión
de ciegas paradojas,
pero la luz en las tinieblas
resplandece como un hilo
pues las huellas de Dios
no se han borrado del camino.

XIII

Viajero:
al caminar te vas desvaneciendo
vas anulando obligaciones
con el tiempo,
para volver a encontrarte
con tus pasos.
En tu dolor
de criatura pasajera
juegas a las escondidas
con tu sino,
pasatiempo de niños inocentes,
pero encauzado
como roca en la existencia.

Viajero:
tú vas pasando unido a los caminos
como embarcaciones huérfanas
que cruzan invisibles
por la bruma,
dejando una imagen que se borra
como un suspiro de esperanza
dejando un vacío que se forma
en un enorme nudo
en la garganta.

XIV

Conocedor del rostro
del camino:
te mueves entre esperanza
partida en diminutos gajos,
y flaquezas que reposan
en la palma de tu mano;
entre una fe que se renueva
cada veinticuatro campanadas
y la duda que te zarandea
como el viento
a la caña en el desierto.
Así caminas tú,
viajero hermano.

En el camino habitas
y en el camino mueres
muchas veces de ansiedades.
¿Qué propósito persiguen
tus miradas?
¿Acaso buscas un amor
que a Dios se le ha perdido?
¿No eres acaso tú ese amor
y andas en busca de ti mismo?
¿Por qué persistes en forjar
fronteras arbitrarias?
¿Acaso para que algún sentido
tenga tu esperanza?

De tu porción de vida
a tu porción de muerte
hay lapsos
deliberadamente ambiguos;
pero la última muerte
es un punto y aparte
solamente,
hacia la plenitud
de un amanecer desconocido,

al cual te vas acercando
sin sentirlo,
a cada jornada de tu sangre
a cada suspiro de la noche
a cada latido de una estrella
a cada vuelta de la misma tierra.

XV

allí vas otra vez
migrante
forjando cultura
con tu mirada
hacia adelante

el sol
ostenta sus sinrazones
que desgarran
tu alma desgarrada

mientras tú pasas
como ancestro viviente
hacia otra tierra ...

segregando su orgullo
el día se alza
con su corona
de omnipotente vuelo

mientras tú pasas
como ancestro viviente
hacia otra tierra ...

la tarde
te da un abrazo fuerte
con siniestras intenciones

y casi queda derretido
el equilibrio
de tu rumbo

mientras tú pasas
como ancestro viviente
hacia otra tierra ...

infalible
el ocaso
cumple con su misión
de darle al sol
debida sepultura
y se dispone a esperar
la resurrección
de su adversario

mientras tú pasas
como ancestro viviente
hacia otra tierra ...

llega la noche
como enlutada viuda
con pasos mudos
jactanciosa
desdeñando los halagos
de los astros
que parpadean a lo lejos

mientras tú pasas
como ancestro viviente
hacia otra tierra ...

XVI

y tú regresas siempre al mismo punto
de la desilusión
de la esperanza
donde comienzas
donde acabas
surges de nuevo y declinas
y queda siempre en el aire
una memoria sin alas

desde que estabas en el vientre
flotando a oscuras
tienen un límite tus acontecimientos
en la tierra
barreras establecidas
con riguroso criterio

sin embargo
ya palpitaba en tu sangre
la esperanza
tu cuerpo
tu cerebro
te piden algo que no hay en ti
y no puedes seguir de un punto ya determinado

te pones a enumerar
las penas que recuerdas
sientes miedo lástima frío
y ganas de estallar en llanto
y ganas de saltar hacia el vacío
frágiles estructuras
son tus pensamientos
llenos de prodigios y de horrores

hay una quietud en el camino
algo ansía liberarse
de la cadena perpetua
del ciclo que desgaja a rebanadas
el perfil humano de tu vida

encuentro inevitable
forcejeos comprometidos
dos fuerzas adversas
a muerte se desgreñan
pero tú impones al final
tu peso de criatura trascendente

"barro serás vencido
aunque me mates con tus golpes
y yo por fin me libraré
de todas mis prisiones"

XVII

Migrante caminante
como si cumplieras
la misma profecía
en cada viaje
tú vas y vienes
por esos ciegos caminos
tú vas y vienes
como por desdoblados
laberintos
cuyos secretos
celosos están
de su prestigio.

Migrante caminante
de tu pecho cuelgan
dos pesadas cadenas
que te sujetan
al seno de la tierra
y persistes como una gota
de agua milenaria
y guardas la costumbre
de las olas que no cesan.

Migrante caminante
eres como fantasma
empolvado en el camino
tu vida es no más pasar ...
pasar ... y siempre pasar ...
pero ... ¿quién verá las huellas
de todo ese caminar?

XVIII

te colmaron de promesas
y tu corazón puso manos a la obra
se dedicó a recoger lo que otros esparcieron
hizo su residencia en la soledad
y vagó muchas noches ocultando su vuelo
y sólo encontró viento y arena
y sendas desconectadas
sangraba poco a poco
a gotas desveladas
edificando piedra sobre piedra
su templo de valores
pero los que te hicieron caminar
fijaron límites abruptos
como cuando se corta la existencia
con voces apagadas
con golpes destructores
y se desmoronó tu templo de valores
al lado de una caricia
hallaste una inquietud
al otro lado de la inquietud
una lluvia de signos y amenazas
y después de la lluvia
surgió de nuevo la esperanza

XIX

Migrante,
vas caminando en el silencio
como vapor humano
        que se prolonga en el tiempo...
espantando recuerdos
        que te persiguen obstinados,
fabricando universos
        que acaso jamás encuentren tus miradas,
debilitando tu fe
        con ansiedades.

    A cada paso el camino es distinto.
    A cada paso el camino es el mismo.

    Migrante,
tu caminar es el de hormigas sonámbulas
        que exploran secretos inauditos.
A mitad del camino
        te asedian visiones poderosas.
En un abrir y cerrar de ojos
        mundos grandiosos se desploman.
Como golondrinas instantáneas
        tus visiones se acercan y se van.
Pasa un abismo momentáneo
        y tu esperanza se reintegra con el viento;
olor a fuego en el desierto
        tristezas añejas
seres queridos que se quedaron dormidos en el tiempo;
        tu corazón da media vuelta
pero tu cuerpo no responde
        pues la necesidad te pinta espejismos en el aire
y te llama de un lugar inconfundible
        de cuyo nombre no quieres ni acordarte.

    A cada paso el camino es distinto.
    A cada paso el camino es el mismo.

>   Migrante,
> queriendo ser generosa
>   la noche te ofrece un sarape de escarcha,
> tu soledad se puebla de sueños dispersos
>   imágenes desfilan por la pista escueta.
> A lo lejos, relámpagos,
>   como fragmentos de futuras vivencias
> vislumbres de otra realidad que anhelas
>   cuyo arquitecto y constructor
> es tu corazón dispuesto a todo.
>   Para ver lo que te espera, cierras los ojos
> dejas ir un suspiro sin que nadie te vea
>   te encomiendas a Dios y dices:
> "Lo que ha de ser que sea,
>   creer es confirmar la sustancia de todas las
>   promesas,"
>
> vas caminando en el silencio
> como vapor humano
>   que se prolonga en el tiempo ...

XX

adversidades
hierven por tus venas
como motivos turbulentos
como ansias impulsadas
por la furia
de muchos huracanes
acumulación de cansancio
en la débil armanzón
de tu conciencia
y como siempre
aparece un recodo
en el camino
tu espíritu
destartalado se complace

algo de fortaleza
parece provenir
del horizonte
que nunca muestra
su carácter verdadero

el sol va agonizando
dejando intacta
su costumbre de morirse
las nubes van buscando
sus orígenes remotos
la brisa se confunde
con el sendero de sus ecos
quién sabe
qué tendrá ese ambiente
su soledad
con nada se compara
el ritual de la noche
hace acto de presencia
nuevamente

algo inexplicable
en la quietud se manifiesta
una región oscura de tu mundo
impone ciertas condiciones
se hace un pacto
en la extensión de un momento
todo se cumple en el acto
salen sobrando
los gestos conocidos
se sincronizan
todas las posibles
concesiones
todo tu ser entra en reposo
y sueñas
y sueñas muchas cosas

la rueda del tiempo
queda detenida
no sucede nada
y sin embargo

todo pasa
por fin en un punto sagrado
de ese tiempo
se desvanece
la semejanza al paraíso
se aleja para siempre
como una nave
como un recuerdo que se pierde
como la vida
que se va y no vuelve

desconcierto en la noche
ganas de regresar
quién sabe adónde
de pronto reconoces
que en la experiencia
del camino
los pasos hacia atrás
no se conocen
salen volando
las interrogaciones
vibrando
hacia los cuatro puntos
cardinales
¿por qué pasan
las cosas como pasan?
un instante se diluye
como la voz del tiempo
por los siglos
toda una vida
que se resume en un instante

permaneces sentado
meditando
serenamente
como niño alucinado
¿por cuánto tiempo todavía?
por fin
recoges cada grano
desparramado de esperanza
como un anciano

pordiosero
que con pena recoge
un puñado prodigioso
de migajas
poco a poquito te levantas
titubeando
sin comprender aún
lo que ha pasado
entre tanto
el camino que aún no has caminado
como impaciente compañero
con su presencia
ya te está llamando

XXI

El camino nunca dice:
"¡Hasta aquí!"
Tú vas en él
y él mora en ti;
y tiene que ser así.
Pero el tiempo, mi hermano,
es inhumano,
antisocial y ocioso
y sigue pasando absorto
en su eterno soliloquio.

XXII

con la cara de orgullo moribundo
    la tarde se va resbalando
    lenta hacia el abismo

va flaqueando también la llamarada del sol
    al golpe
    de las tinieblas

en el horizonte se divisan aves nocturnas
    inocentes
    que no se paran a medir distancias

sólo pasan volando, como tú, migrante hermano
    sólo pasan volando
    por el camino

el tiempo te transporta en su nave alegórica
    y el viento lleva a cuestas
    desgracias infinitas

a la distancia el silencio murmura sus misterios
    y tu alma se acopla
    a los ecos de la noche

y sigues pasando, migrante hermano
    y sigues pasando
    por el camino ...

XXIII

Te veo caminando, migrante,
y me pregunto:
        ¿Qué número, de sueño,
calzan tus pies mal entendidos?
        ¿Qué proporción de geografía
entra en tus ojos casi ausentes?
        ¿De qué tamaño es la simiente
que guarda tu corazón para estas ocasiones?

XXIV

Párate, migrante,
a contemplar bien el paisaje
pues ya no pasarás, jamás,
por este mismo sitio
en este mismo momento de tu historia,
aunque sea el camino
el mismo compañero,
será un camino nuevo—
la presencia de lo desconocido.

Párate, migrante,
a contemplar bien el paisaje
a recogerte dentro de ti mismo;
tú pasas diligente
pero el camino queda.

Huellas frescas
visiones que no mueren
nuevas palpitaciones
en las encrucijadas de caminos viejos,
nacen alternativas
en senderos desaparecidos;
surge un afán de revivir

la sangre que has perdido
en el pulso secreto de todos
los recuerdos
que se confunden
con el fluir de momentos venideros.

XXV

tus gotas de sudor
riegan el vientre de la tierra
y ella se siente amada
al toque de tus manos
una promesa brota
desde el fondo
una razón que no se nombra
cobra vida
en momento propicio
ella entrega sus frutos sin recelo
como madre abnegada
repartidora de esperanzas
frutos que deberían de ser tuyos
que por torcidos documentos
que por caprichos francamente obscenos
a otros pertenecen

la tierra y tú
han sido quemados muchas veces
de tantos salvajes menosprecios
entre un viaje y otro viaje
habitas con ella íntimamente
después recoges sus frutos bien habidos
y sigues tu camino
hasta las otras pizcas

por ahora ese es tu privilegio
tu sola recompensa
pero llegará el día

y ya se acerca
en que un vástago retoñará
de las raíces de la tierra
trayendo en su cintura la justicia
y acontecerá también en aquel día
que sobre toda la faz de la tierra
se cumplirán las promesas antiguas

Real Poetría

El Huitlacoche

El Huitlacoche is the nom de plume of Gary D. Keller. The name was selected for—among others—at least two reasons: its symbolic significance as a food eaten by the pre-Columbian mesoamericanos (it is a fungus that grows symbiotically with corn) and because it was the apodo of a well-known Mexican boxer who was much loved on the border during his youth not only as a pugilist but as a benefactor of the poor. Of Mexican ancestry on his mother's side and of American on his father's, Keller was born in 1943 and raised almost literally on the border, casi con un pie en cada estribo.

During his youth his family made a living by hauling scrap metal, particularly lead batteries and tin cans, across the border from the United States into Mexico, converting it into ingots, and reselling it in the United States. This was a quasi-legal and adventuresome operation and they found themselves typically traveling the border in pursuit of metamorphosible metal from National City, California, to as far east as El Paso. Keller had a highly peripatetic schooling until high school (when his father secured a more stable job), although he is grateful for two years with the Discalced Carmelites (but not for their forcing him to change from left-handedness to right-handedness). An omnivorous reader, he educated himself basically with junkyard finds, typically the women's magazines of the 1950s (can this marriage be saved? his version, her version, the counselor's position) with some Dostoyevsky and other high literature thrown in.

Keller spent his youth bringing in chavos for the family, working at such things as scrap metal hauler, molinero de nixtamal, entrenador de gansos industriales, gumball machine mechanic, and door-to-door egg salesman. Recreation consisted of hanging around with his motorcycle gang or mixing it up with sailors in National City bars. He attended the Universidad de las Américas and supported himself by teaching English in Mexico City. After receiving a B.A. in Philosophy, he was awarded a fellowship in creative writing at Columbia University, where ultimately he received a Ph.D.

At present he is the Provost at SUNY-Binghamton. He is married and has three children; the two youngest are cuatitos. His story "The Man Who Invented the Automatic Jumping Bean" was selected as one of the best stories published by the small presses in 1977.

Publications Related to Chicano Studies

Creative Literature

"The Man Who Invented the Automatic Jumping Bean" (short story).
   Bilingual Review, I, 2 (1974). Reprinted in *The Pushcart Prize, II: Best
   of the Small Presses,* ed. Bill Henderson. New York: Pushcart Press,
   1977; and *Best of the Small Presses,* ed. Bill Henderson. New York:
   Avon Books, 1977.
"From the Heights of Macho Bicho," "¡Hostias!" (poetry). *Bilingual
   Review*, II, Nos. 1 & 2 (1975).
"The Urban(e) Chicano's 76" (poetry). *Bilingual Review*, III, No. 3 (1976).
"Searching for La Real Cosa" (poetry). *Bilingual Review*, V, Nos. 1 & 2
   (1978).
"By Waterbug Beloved" (poetry). In *Hispanics in the United States: An
   Anthology of Creative Literature,* ed. Gary D. Keller and Francisco
   Jiménez. Ypsilanti, MI: Bilingual Press, 1980, 137-40.
"Mocha in Disneyland" (short story). In *Hispanics in the United States:
   An Anthology of Creative Literature,* ed. Gary D. Keller and Francisco
   Jiménez. Ypsilanti, MI: Bilingual Press, 1980, 57-74.
"The Mojado Who Offered Up His Tapeworms to the Public Weal" (short
   story). In *Hispanics in the United States: An Anthology of Creative
   Literature, Vol. II,* ed. Francisco Jiménez and Gary D. Keller.
   Ypsilanti, MI: Bilingual Press, 1982, 13-27.
Tales of El Huitlachoche (short stories). Colorado Springs, CO: Maize
   Press, 1984.

Research and Scholarship

Bilingualism in the Bicentennial and Beyond (with Richard V. Teschner
   and Silvia Viera). New York: Bilingual Press, 1976.
Bilingual Education for Hispanic Students in the United States (with
   Joshua A. Fishman). New York: Teachers College Press of Columbia
   University, 1981.
"The Systematic Exclusion of the Language and Culture of Boricuas,
   Chicanos, and Other U.S. Hispanos in Elementary Spanish Grammar
   Textbooks Published in the United States." *Bilingual Review*, I, 3
   (Sept.-Dec. 1974), 227-235.
"Psychological Stress Among Speakers of United States Vernacular
   Spanish." In Luis Ortega, ed., *Introduction to Bilingual Education.*
   New York: Las Américas-Anaya, 1975.
"Toward a Stylistic Analysis of Bilingual Texts: From Ernest Hemingway
   to Contemporary Boricua and Chicano Literature." In Mary A. Beck,
   et al., eds., *The Analysis of Hispanic Texts: Current Trends in
   Methodology.* New York: Bilingual Press, 1976.

"Acquisition of the English and Spanish Passive Voices Among Bilingual Children." In Gary D. Keller, Richard V. Teschner, and Silvia Viera, *Bilingualism in the Bicentennial and Beyond.* New York: Bilingual Press, 1976.

"Bilingualism and Bilingual Education in the United States: A Chronology from the Colonial Period to 1976" (pamphlet; with Karen S. Van Hooft). New York: Bilingual Press, 1976.

"French-Canadian Secessionism and the Crisis of Bilingual Education in the United States." *Bilingual Review,* Vol. IV, Numbers 1 & 2 (Jan.-Aug. 1977), 1-6.

"The Literary Stratagems Available to the Bilingual Chicano Writer." In Francisco Jiménez, ed., *The Identification and Analysis of Chicano Literature.* New York: Bilingual Press, 1979, 263-316.

"The Ultimate Goal of Bilingual Education With Respect to Language Skills." In *Bilingual Education for Hispanic Students in the United States,* ed. Joshua A. Fishman and Gary D. Keller. New York: Teachers College Press of Columbia University, 1981, 68-81.

"Alurista, el antropólogo and the Recuperation of the Chicano Identity." Introduction to Alurista, *Return: Poems Collected and New.* Ypsilanti, MI: Bilingual Press, 1981, ix-xviii.

"What Can Language Planners Learn From the Hispanic Experience with Corpus Planning in the United States?" In Juan Cobarrubias and Joshua A. Fishman, eds., *Progress in Language Planning: International Perspectives.* The Hague: Mouton, 1983, 253-265.

Searching for La Real Cosa

Sel o no sel,
that is the lío.
(Emilio Díaz Valcárcel,
        *Figuraciones en el
                mes de marzo*)

¿Quién es La Real Cosa?
¡Dime, dime por favor!

Is it radical chic,
the poverty pimp
who mouthed nasties at Berkeley-by-the-Sea
and teaches chic studies
at Foothill Comm Coll?
Or is it Huitla's papi
who invented the automatic jumping bean
from an empty contac capsule
and a ball of pusillanimous mercury?
Is it el vato loco, man?
Roaring into downtown vegas tight
on his skull and bones cycle
sousing himself to perdición
on gabo's gratis spirits
at the well-lit crap table
while he tarries for the man
to develop his picture and
his querida—two brown persons
standing tween one million laminated smackers
como el Cristo plastificado entre los dos ladrones.
Or is it el pueta de la Raza scoring big
a grant from the feds to bring
a florid festival to la Raza?
His prettiest Chicana gets to wear
the poet's garland round her head
while he stalks the stage
dressed in a maiden-formed Jaguar suit
and a wooden club we used for stickball
muttering darkly about the sun and blood—

he's no hemophiliac
a rezar todos a Don Huitzilopochtli
por la venida del quinto sol.

¿Quién es La Real Cosa?
¡Dime, dime, por amor de Dios!

I believe, conceding the purely ad hoc validity of such generalizations, that
in the last decade the net increase of *Raza* machos who go down on their
hembras is a significant statistic on the road to consummated *Aztlán*. It's
good to have a plan for the future, particularly when it builds upon the
achievements of the past. And it's best to begin in the home.

Once they gave us a test to see
if we were bilingual
Look into the binoculars
fixed onto the wall:

Dime	Dime
Pan	Pan
Hay	Hay
Sea	Sea
Once	Once
Pie	Pie

Is this a binary hoodwink?
Schizophrenia or stereoscopy?
¿mala fe? or merely ¿mala leche?
Each clicking of the frame
the data base is shifting
stirring up
profound malaise
maladicta—mal de siècle
Shit!
I'm only bilingual
I don't got double vision

¿Quién es La Real Cosa?
la cosa nuestra
la cosa nostra
(be careful about doing your thing
before I can say ok
I've got to know your thing)

¡Dime, dime por amor de Dios!
Poor Huitlacito
Something's awry in his head.
He does not take la Tequila
He prefers Johnny Walker instead.
He's no Tío Taco y menos tirilón
He's no regalado y menos un rajón
But he missed out on chic studies
        at San José State
and he reads Lamb and Hazlitt
                for pleasure
and prefers Remedio's unsullied bedsheets
to the contrafraternity of the golden carp
Sometimes he goes around the country
(the suburbs and the urbs)
and senses
he's foni.

In Mexico exist scholars who define el Chicano as an "hijo de la chingada"
on the road to becoming a "son of a bitch." A falta de pan, de tierra y de
libertad, hay mexicanos que se cobijan en su soberbia.

Dime, manito del alma, ¿eres tú la gran cosa?
Vamos, panín, ¿eres hijo de la gran puta
o gran hijo de algo?
You say potato and I say patata
You say sweet potato and I say batata
You say macho and I say hembra
You say marimacho and I say marijuana
You say "voy a coger esa guagua"
and I say "quisiera coger esa prieta"
Let's call the whole thing off!

Chicano Spanish is heavily into ch.

First of all there's: chágüer (shower), chain (shine), champion,
                             champú, chat (French for gato, Chicano for
                             injection), checar, chérbit (I prefer lime), cherife,
                             cho, choc, chot (var. of chat, but doesn't mean
                             gato, even in French), and chusear.

and there's:	chicanada, chicanear, chicaneo, chicanería, chicanismo, chicanglo (Chicano who acts like Anglo), chicabacho (see chicanglo, but worse).
and how about:	chale (prick), chalito (prick, but smaller), chicote (prick, a pretty large one, cf. chiquito), chile (potentially ambiguous; prick, especially if the chile is parado rather than piquín, in which case it's merely a very piquant caper-sized red pepper), chiludo (prick, a really big one, both the man and his prick, ¡Huy, qué envidia!), chorizo (prick, but also good for Spanish omelettes), chingada, chin su (or tu, depending on degree of intimacy) ma (very strong and vulgar, f____ y____ m____!), chingadazo (never a thing to do with sex, strictly violence), chingadera, chingal (a lot, plenty), chingatal (see supra., only a lot more), chingazo, chingos, chinguiza, chingón: el mero chingón (similar to la gran cosa, la real cosa, el gran queso, mandamás, mandamás de todos los mandamases, capo, capo de tutti capi, etc.) chichi (tit, also soft work, like what poverty pimps do), chichón (tit, but a lot bigger, counterpart to chiludo, v. supra.), chapetuda (woman sexually with it), chapetear (f____), chingar (f____), and ¡Chive! (Don't be frightened!)
I don't mean to detain you but these are interesting too:	Chabela (Isabel), Chago (Santiago), Chale (Carlos, also prick, remember?), Chalito (Carlos, but a smaller prick), Challo (Rosario), Chano (Feliciano, Graciano, Luciano), Chayo (Eduardo), Chela (Graciela, Celia), Chelo (Consuelo), Chencho/Chencha (Cresencio, Cresencia), Chente/Chenta (Vicente, Vicenta), Chito/Chita (Jesús, Jesusa; Felicito, Felicita), Chon/Chona (Asunción, Encarnación, Concepción), Chucho (Jesús, María de Jesús, but also means sly, astute, foxy, and dog).

¡Charamba! I guess that just about sums up the notion of Chicano semantic fields!

> Por fin, ¿eh? ¡Ya estuvo!
> ¿Quién es la real cosa?
> A dime, dime for the love of God!

¡Mangos! Esa cosa no soy yo.
¡Madre! Ese vato, ¡qué sé yo!
I'm just a cunning lingual
I no got stereoscopic vision.

The Urban(e) Chicano's 76

Pues, I'm just a vato loco man
but if I had my way again
I'd ask for 'Miliano Zapata's rise
Steinbeck claims he never died
I crave that dude at my side
I'd deal him aces at Circus-Circus
under the glazed gaze of the pit boss
Man, I'd drag him to the Catskills
learn him all my washing dish skills
We'd sing Mex war songs like 30-30
drink a little and talk some dirty,
Oh yeah, we'd besport like meros machos
make it with couple of blondas gabachas
I'd take you see a double flick
¡Viva Zapata! and *Wild One!*—what you think?
Maybe we'd take dead John's advice
learn ourselves to read and write.

If I had Zapata
I'd take him to the chili-bean-bicentennial
contest in Arlington, Texas
and to the Trade Center tower
to see the guard rail that don't
let them go over the side.
If I had Zapata at my side
I'd take him to lower Berkeley-by-the-Bay
a vast massagehouse greased on Master Charge
and leaf the *Barb* and upchuck
and Stanford, the gabacho's Alhambra

and Crystal City ¡Motherfucker!
where Chicanos run the show
and to New Mex Highlands Univer
for a course on contAmerlit
Zapata comes out on the wedding night
in pajama bottoms, he yearns to read and write
I love you Johnny, the way you write
but shit, you stink, babosísimo fool
that's my boy up there in striped bottoms
addressing armed campesinos in broad-brimmed sombreros
from the balcony railing with Arabesques
        ¡el frito bandito!
national symbol
Watergate bi-sentinel
bilingual's lingual the cunning lingual
he's the speaker
here's the man.

So who's up for 76?
I'm up for anything.
I'm running for alderperson
on the Zapata-Chávez ticket
I'm running for keeper
at the Amer Revol Bicent Admin
I'm bilingual so I can mingle
I'm bicultural so I can cut it
I'm bisexual so I'll hex it
I wanna run the show
where they keep tabs
on every podunk blip
in this banal body politic
that's gonna do heritage, festival and horizons
Horizons ¡madre! eso es preciso
So, pues, I'm just a vato loco man
but if we have our way again
we'll ask for 'Miliano Zapata's rise
stake him out in pater-frater's guise
cause if we have Zapata
We'll never again need Zapata.

From the Heights of Macho Bicho

Pa' don Pablo Neruda

From the heights of Macho Bicho
To the shores of Tonkin Bay...

All I need say is
Fock US marines
pero benditos seamos los marine tigers
apetecedores de moles y alcapurrias
y el ensueño de la olla uniforme
a uniform aggression.
O the slick and seductive
Tío Sam
chivote barbudo
con su guiño de déspota paternal
y el dedo meñique
¿Remember US
batting black label beer cans over the barda
at Guantánamo
while Fidel Castro Ruz
refunfuñaba por las tierras
alzando los cojones de Martí
como de cocos los tenía
el pobre pueta
de lo apóstol que era?

Fock ain't what you tink.
It's a question of words.
Even the dolphin has its register.

On Accounta Inc.
I hold no stock in you.
You turned el chile into preprocessed velveeta
and Tiburcio Vásquez into el frito bandito
You made Emiliano Zapata
Marlon Brando who went to bed
in his pajama bottoms on the wedding night.

On Accounta Inc.
De mi parte
Como pueta
Tell US marines
que aquí 'tamos nomás
a las justas alturas
de las circunstancias
con el quetzal y la anaconda
los de bicho alto
y los de palo alto
aquí nomás nomás
We're waiting for US marines
los meros justos
los justos meros
los meros meros
los meros machos
los mandamás.

My Man, Bobby K, Lying in the Kitchen

(on the 10th anniversary)

Yo gone and done it, my man
just for us in gabo's kitchen

Hang hard, my man
to those loose leafs of history
yo pilgrim of peace
spawned from jism
gone to ism.

I'm minding the carcass of the chameleon people
this monarch of the monads
acme of demos.

How life ceases like a lonely ballad
in a homespun and endmost Folsom

Life colored by puff and pop
The pop of a bubbletop
The pop of the weasels
The pop of soda shook and gushing

I'm surely sad to mind yo dead
I wanted so to kiss yo head
so I kissed yo grave instead
and gone to Bed-Sty
to mark your name
after 10 I'm still in pain

So hang on my man
to such history what yo still got
Livid transfixion on exanimate living
Life lifted to the loft of Logos
Be! Yo hear?
Be the Wizard of wa Is!

By Waterbug Beloved

So you deigned derision
when I reported the waterbug
was simply waiting
for you to fall sound asleep
to approach your person
to scuttle up the platform bed
to march up your alabaster calf
your snowy-white thigh
to introduce itself into your asshole
and nestle there, warm
amidst the fecal plenty
god knows, even
to deposit its otherly larvae.

¿Qué pasa, Huitla? she asks
Got a bug up your ass?

Conjuring up spells from the netherlife
to torment yourself and loved ones?
He who suffers from Quixotitis.
Lock the bedroom door or not
Stuff the door-crack with magazines
and brown bags if you must
Tie a rag round your ass or better
don your jock
do it—frankly I give a flying fuck
only lie still for chrissake
and allow me the solace of my sleep.

No, woman, you fool me not one whit!
You're nohow like that self
a week ago
that slept like a cat in oestrus
a squirrel-monkey in her submissive pose
the pillow down by your navel
your ass propped up and ripe
enough to make a man's steadfast anchor
rouse and rise from Davy Jones' Locker
so wondering what transpired
when in the morning you found
your panties down round your ankles.

Now lie snoring, weird whistlings
emerging from you like taps and valves
modulating in the nasal passage
Why are you drawn up like fetus
and not in warm embrace
with the sponge-rubber pillow?
I say you're protecting your ass!
Why are you making whining sounds
like you were a dog or
living out reverie, moaning away
reformulating one nightmare, or more,
a craven whim gone sour,
redoing the scavenge or the hunt?

Last night I had to pee
and walked the dark narrow hall

on the way to peepeeporium
my arm brushed by the scuttling otherlife
I'm not likely to forget contact
one fleeting feeling
on the hair follicles
the shock and suddenness of it—
a violation.
I couldn't liquidate it,
even with the hall light burning,
Time magazine folded like a bludgeon
it fled into the lightless recess
by the side of the fridge.

Tonight I need to pee again
my wife is whirring and dreaming
of the beasties of the night
the kids, way up the defiled corridor
past all excuse, alone, dead in their pallets
the Spic's pointed shoes
lie lifeless in the corner
So what's a guy to do?

My poor sons
I would save you from heavy traffic
I would push you afield
and swoon before a Datsun pickup
if necessary
just out of paternal impulse
but this premeditated duty of waterbugs
a black conch-shelled ens
that sits in its orb of sultry squalor
punctilious as a creditor
an accuser from down low
is enough to unnerve an honorable soul.

So the Hispanic father
dons tight-fitting shorts
a baseball cap to guard his hair
a tightly rolled mag and a flashlight,
ventures out
gingerly shaking newspapers and bags

from the space under the door.
Like Quixote he sallies forth
first to the children's quarters
where his primogenital duty rests,
then to kitchen, bathroom, and parlor,
there is nothing
nada
mierda
his children are sleeping open-mouthed
moon-faced before the swift incision of light
all orifices relaxed
at peace with nature.
There is not one waterbug
not even a cucaracha
not even a housefly
there is simply the swelter of night
and all the likely nestings
stark in white light as sin itself
fuzzy-wuzzies in the corners of the corridor
a grease stain on the kitchen floor
where the juice of meats
has oozed from the broiler
the leaky faucet that would provide
oasis for a shelled Beelzebub.
Unrequited, papa takes off his cap
puts papers in place under the door
The underpants feel tight and raspy
on his prone body
his bladder is empty, his sex has shrunk
into the cup of his jockey shorts.

So then, where does this bugger lurk?
This lightless life unbounded
like a symptom we simply endure
an erection, a pee-swollen penis,
a distended sex
lurking in the sports page
of the *L.A. Times*
nibbling flakes and crumbs of tortilla chips
wiping her black chops with her filaments
bathing in the milk carton in the garbage

while unheeding we put out the garbage
nestled comfy in the waxy vessel
her dark frail legs an unseemly primadonna
dipping into the milk of our life.

Love Poem With a Guilty Rider

Under the awning of the shortening shadow
Unawed the arching foliage spoke
Do you advocate the artichoke
                    or follow the avocado?
I peered at your incarnate wish
You peered into the penumbra.

So now, do you love me
When the bed freezes over
and the mirror sprouts horns?
I do and so relieved that it is done!

Along the arcade of this analogic
recessed in trim revelation
your foreribbed innocence
miscuing the onus of idols
appending your sinuous omniscience
with time.
The ark is tiny and timely
transversing
the hemsex of history
by crosshairs of carbines
triggered to rigging
the calloused cupronickel key
sheathing the lit ignition
quad barrel twin carbs
savoring the salt of Bensonhurst
long maiden lanes of reborne Brooklyn

bearing boroughs and reborn heights.
It's an ingrown trip
Set back and rotate.

So now, do you love me
When is is nothing is?
I preferred to let it lay
as Husserl, in epoché.

I recognate
footing in festive rite
beneath the delineate lunar roundel
along the elm-serried channel
legging the crosstauts of my doubleribbed desire
Death and desire, the ambience
of amorous omnipotence, sealed
the twin imprint, an eclipse
or ordinate and inordinate hegemony.
I desired you
for myself.

Suddenly
under the aura
of a circumvallate orality
your person returned to lips
tuned to the tenure of my tongue
spread pith by tasty pith
the outer folds and inner lips
turn transparent.
My penis rose like an ikon
from a limbo of promontories
honed to your palpate of schisms
piercing the umbra of my sullen content
til the cowl reopened to morning
begetting my reposited plum

I've recome
to beseed the staff of my rent and refused son
Realizing
the querulous inquest we've bereaved begun
So relieved that it is done!

Love Poem

Sun which forms the fruit
ripens earth a flaxen seed
spreads the tender wood
soft leaf and ripe timid berry.

A blazing cluster lights your person
the veined leaf rises to sun
Within your person summer leaves
turn a fluted song.

Rhetoric de la chingada

Pretty pechos dear
Pretty pechos speak to me
your forsworn conjurations
your unchecked climax cleft
your mounting thrusting
renting maiden swell;
culled shell, clasped and
cowled pith supplely spurs
my scandent swift incision.

All around the mulberry bush
the monkey goes a sniffing
As once said Herodes
o te chingas o te jodes.

Forefixed formal fusion
this form freely foaled,
bowed her sheaf fulfilled flesh
and bore a fallow firmament;
rent and reformed rib, twin star
staunch nil sidled fire
riven from our fierce elation

¡The Annunciation!

Body bound, belly bound
breasts bound and brought to heart,
forget it, hombre
sunk in her soundless shaft
she is plumbed ponderous
upon her onerous sameness
an indrawn star
set in veerless parabolas
unminded, insensate, foreclosed.

Let it die, my man
Remove your firm, obdurate other
Tell her your fairy tale
and close on its climax
juntos pero no revueltos.

The Amphibian

Thou terrapin turned diadem back
to sandy lap of wanton reminiscence
Slipped thy crypt as clam
Bared thy shy being bather
dunked baleful flipper in thine garnish
dropped bit of ova on granules.

Tapped auricles to her lapped dampened rise
and bay of piscine wolverine
beneath trilled trough
her willful shadow.

Natural Order

The shrill state squirrels
of pigeons pose
genuflect to amber weed
yield in dull ether
leaves curled or taut
whirl thin reeds
dead. Moribund

Day to night wears
the tipped horned moon
sonata eve tops
crowns of worn bark

Galactic

The little boy dabbed milk
at the tip of his dick   .
to let the cat lick
lactic ribbed her chalky rasping
Sand papered flesh
her sleek caress.

An almond ringed
by flaxen glyphs and serum
posed the while musing
the milk of my life.

¡Hostias!

Nowadays
I down my wafer
with peanut butter and jelly
spread thin
from the selfsame striped jar
mm mm good, mm mm good
A latter day proof
of the one-in-many God.

Just one second!
Isn't the three-in-one concept
a very fine steak sauce?
Or maybe a useful
lubricating oil?
You never know
when you might find yourself
in
a tight spot.

¡Ay Bendito!

I have turned towards God
to myself
For I no longer endure
it, my manhood
thus I thrust
it on my model
at my God
upon myself.

Judaica Chicana

Sem Tob, the master,
Proverbios morales
(1350-1369)

El Huitlacoche's Respectful
Translation

Cuando es seca la rosa,
que ya su sazón sale,
queda el agua olorosa,
rosada, que más vale.

When the rose is dry
its spice undone
the rose water stays,
so fragrantly.

*   *   *

*   *   *

Por nacer en espino
la rosa, yo no siento
que pierde, nin el buen vino
por salir del sarmiento.
Nin vale el azor menos
porque en vil nido siga,
nin los ejemplos buenos
porque judio los diga.

Though rose of spines is born
I know she is unweakened
nor full wine, even
from the vine shoot torn.
Nor the hawk unlofty
in keeping with her nest
nor true examples blackened
when practiced by a Jew.

The Reason People Don't Like Mexicans

Leroy V. Quintana

Leroy V. Quintana was born in Albuquerque, New Mexico, on June 10, 1944, but spent his formative years with his grandparents in Ratón, New Mexico. They spoke virtually no English, so he was told all the old stories—the *cuentos*, with their simple but deep understanding of the world—in Spanish. His grandmother would recount stories of her past as she made candy on the old firewood stove, and his grandfather would tell the stories of his youth—of walking to Wyoming to shear sheep on the large ranchos there, tales of the characters in the sheep camps, of the land he lost. When they died, an entire way of life was lost with them.

Quintana graduated from Albuquerque High School, enrolled at the University of New Mexico, joined the Army, went to jump school, got to see Georgia, and then toured Vietnam by chopper and by foot while in recon. He returned alive and in one piece, at least physically, married, finished his B.A. in English at the University of New Mexico, worked as an alcoholism caseworker, and then decided to go to graduate school. He received his M.A. in English from New Mexico State University in Las Cruces and taught there for a year. He then moved to El Paso and taught at El Paso Community College, later returning to Albuquerque.

He is currently a lecturer in the English Department at the University of New Mexico. He has two daughters, Sandra, 10, and Elisa, 8. He has published two books of poems and in 1978 won a National Endowment for the Arts Creative Writing Fellowship.

Publications

Books

Hijo del Pueblo: New Mexico Poems, 1974
Sangre. Las Cruces, NM: Prima Agua Press, 1981.

Poems in Anthologies

Voices From the Rio Grande, The Indian Rio Grande, Passing Through, Chicano Voices, 101 Poets of the 60's and 70's, Anthology of Magazine Verse and Yearbook of American Poetry-1979, Southwest, Anuario de Letras Chicanas/Latinoamericanas, A Geography of Poets, Hispanics in the United States: An Anthology of Creative Literature

Poems in Periodicals

The Wormwood Review, The Pawn Review, The Sunstone Review, Dacotah Territory, Green Horse for Poetry, Poetry Texas, New Mexico Magazine, Puerto del Sol, San Marcos Review, Revista Chicano-Riqueña, Sailing the Roadclear, Texas Portfolio, New America, Colorado State Review, La Confluencia, Nuestro, Phantasm, River Styx, New Mexico Humanities Review, The Greenfield Review, The American Poetry Review, Latin American Literary Review, Contact II, Tejidos.

I. The Reason People Don't Like Mexicans

Because We Were Born To Get Our Ass Kicked

Rule Number One of the barrio states
never let anyone
kick it for free, otherwise
he'll think it's his
to do, whenever
and ever.

José Mentiras says that a Chicano
sometimes has to do a lot of walking backwards
in order to go forward

When he was young
he'd wait outside the movie theater
until the crowds came out
then he'd sneak in, walking backwards

The ushers never noticed him
and says you'd be surprised
how the people walking out
will even get out of your way

Don José worked as a woodcutter once,
had his own team and carro de caballos.
Once, another man, who had neither
horses nor wagon, a man he didn't know
was his friend or his enemy,
told Don José he knew a place
a hundred miles or so to the north
where a box of tesoro was buried
and suggested the two go there
in Don José's wagon and bring it home.

Don José gave some thought
to the man's uncommon offer,
but in the end decided against it—
in all the stories he had ever heard
where two men rode off to find tesoro
in all of them only one ever returned,
with not one word whatsoever
of the wealth they went for,
but with twice as many horses as before.

Rumaldo

Owned the typical corner grocery
Counters cramped into what
would've been the living room
Talked so fast, punctuated
with a quick stutter
It could've been Japanese
Punched and cranked his adding machine
even faster
His eyes two thin squints
behind the thickest of lenses
Nicknamed Japo
he looked exactly like Hirohito

Hot Chile

Don José says Chicanos have suffered so much;
That we're so used to it
we like to suffer
even when we eat.

                    every day
                    he went to communion.
                    always walked
                    up to the altar
                    before the priest
                    came down
                    with the host.
                    even though
                    the nuns
                    had taught us
                    that God
                    had made us all equal
                    we waited until
                    he walked back
                    down the aisle—
                    that huge hole in
                    his forehead
                    from the war or
                    some terrible accident

José Mentiras was putting in a new sewer line
Now it's plastic tubes, quick drying glue
instead of iron pipes with lead and rope for sealers

Amazing what the Anglos think up!
Why we'd still be running around in wagons
with ruedas cuadradas

When Primo Ramón came to visit
smoking a big stogie on a gnarled rubber holder
and dressed in his handsome suit
we would sit and listen so closely
to the stories, his jokes first told in Spanish
then retold in an English without a trace
It sounded strange, even funny
to hear him refer to Anglos as "bolillos"
Such an odd term, especially from him
who with his light complexion and auburn hair
could pass for one so easily
and probably did

Doña María says
People should be proud to be what they are
instead of trying to pass themselves off for what they aren't

The reason people don't like Mexicans
is because Mexicans don't like Mexicans

MacMahon's Grocery

Cokes were ten cents then
It felt both great and petty
to steal from him
An Anglo, after all
And he knew, I'm sure
all our little crimes
Let us go our way
with the delicious, chocolate-covered donuts he sold
those luscious, bitter lemons we stole

José Mentiras was saying he read in the paper
the incidence of colo-rectal cancer
is higher among Anglos than Chicanos

So now the Anglos are conducting
all types of surveys, trying to find out
what makes Chicanos different, the diet, lifestyle

José Mentiras says they're really scared
but can't really blame them
figures they're just trying to save their ass

Más llaves que San Pedro

para Jimmie Aragón,
de Peña Blanca, New Mexico

Stopped at the Texaco Station in Peña Blanca,
asked for three dollars of Regular
and started searching on my key ring
for the one that would open the gas cap.
"Más llaves que San Pedro,"
Jimmie Aragón, the owner, says.
"More keys than Saint Peter."
"And Saint Peter, does he have a lot of keys?"
I ask him in Spanish.
"Creo que sí, él tiene todas las llaves del cielo."
He must, He has all the keys to the kingdom of heaven.
"Y hay de haber muchos cuartos allá 'rriba."
And there's bound to be a hell of a lot of rooms up there.

That summer I was not yet
and Benny was, but only recently;
and so proud as he beat off;
a pocket watch in the other hand;
trying to outdo time again;
under the old bridge

Chicken Feathers

Ask José Mentiras what he had eaten
and he'd tell you proudly "gallina."

Sí, of course, and those dried bean stains
down his shirt front, those were the plumas.

Quizás quería más plomo

pa los compas en Silva's Saloon

Tranquilino and Flavio were talking
about a crazy woman the other day,
the one who shot her husband
full of lead "En el mero garrote"
according to Tranquilino.
"¡Por el mero chile!," adds Flavio,
who saw the man walking down the street,
his groin dripping with blood,
and called the ambulance.
And what happened to the man?
"He lived," explains Flavio.
"He's back with the same woman.
He looks very happy and so does she."
Nobody ever figured out
why she shot him in the first place.
Flavio figures "Que quizás quería más plomo."

José Mentiras can't wait for five o'clock to come around
To go home to the smell of tortillas
being cooked on a hot stove
Says he surprises his wife from behind
and kneads her nalgas
the way she does the dough

Shoveling Manure With Gilbert López

para mi compa Gilbert López

Even shoveling manure with Gilbert López
is an enlightening experience:
a lesson in achieving harmony in marriage.

My shovel is small, heart-shaped,
not especially good for shoveling manure.

Gilbert's is larger, rectangular,
not as big as a large scoop, but broad and deep.

When we trade after shoveling for an hour
and stopping for a beer

I ask what his shovel is called.
A small scoop? A medium scoop?

"That's what's known as an 'Amansador de Burros'"
he says, and I ask why it's named that.

"Because when things aren't going right at home,"
he replies, "and a man can't take it anymore,

he can grab that shovel, get the hell out of there
and go out and shovel all the shit he wants—
until all his problems disappear."

Monday through Saturday
business was Regular
at Chivo's gas station

Sundays meant more Ethyl
Pumped bootleg wine at prices
we now pay for gas

Bet we would've made beautiful babies
blue-eyed girls, brown-brooding boys

Along with front-page, back-fence gossip
for years—in your tongue—and mine.

II. What Can They Do, Send Us to The Nam?

First Night In Viet Nam

Twenty-nine years
and sent to Viet Nam
to retire with thirty.
Full Stars and Stripes benefits forever.
But the Army had been a good provider.

I felt sorry for him
and for the rest of us,
as long after lights out
we began crossing out days.

Some, to get back to the world sooner
threw away their malaria pills

Tried to turn
green as government issue

Came to be known as Combat Smith
His mind a misfire
since that day
he ran out of ammo
swinging his entrenching tool—
The dead Viet Cong
at his feet

Cookie faked seeing some V.C.
quickly crouched low in the tall grass
to radio the choppers to come back

Just missed a punji stake in his balls
Got an embarrassed Purple Heart
pinned next to his
by a major whose sole duty in the Army it was

The lieutenant wanted to see action
prove to himself, the world,
he was more than a punk louie
And in time
the sight of so much death
turned him a lifeless shade of yellow
he wore as proudly as dress khakis

Bates

Was sent out as F.O. that night.

Then his shrill pleas for help
out there in the darkness

where they waited with his screams
tempting screams, until first light,

when his company swept the area.
His skin beside him like a twin brother.

Every morning was gooks and more
gooks, wave after wave of N.V.A.'s
mines strapped to their chests

His detonated eyes, unblinking
We snickered until
Suddenly he stopped talking to himself
Call us to attention
Tell how it was going to be in the Nam

To save our lives, if a way had been his
would've pulled the pin from a grenade
have one in our midst hold it
see if our eyes
so much as blinked with sleep

He understood the mechanics of death
as well as the contradictions of life

could disassemble and assemble any weapon
with the same ease as playing Yankee Doodle

and Dixie simultaneously on the guitar.
The war saddened his solemn eyes forever.

Fourflushed his way
with or without a deck of cards

His head blown away
by a V.C.

walked up behind him
dealt a wild deuce   .

and four of a kind
All bullets

Too bad the lieutenant marched
straight into that Chinese claymore
          rusty bolts and nails
          broken bits of "33" beer bottles
          fragments of G.I. junk
pierced his
          spit shined boots
          pressed fatigues
     his fine, rigid body
died a dirt-cheap, uncombed death

A star even in combat
A face the war would never ugly
So re-upped for six more months
Went home to a parade
The Silver Star of his city

* And when the V.C. zapped him
If him
What of us?

The last he set foot in the Nam
Only a little more than half of him left
His legs still Missing In Action
Even shrapnel so small
seemed like an explosion of blackheads
across his face

If it wasn't the V.C. wanting to blow your shit away
It was the Army insisting this was still the Army

Used to be a saying in Viet Nam:
What can they do—send me to Viet Nam?

Them from The
Big Red 1
said

was
a
bitch

down
in the
Delta

Wet
day and
night

The water
2 feet
high

in the
dry
places.

Stuckey sawed the handle
of his M-79 into a pistol grip
In the boonies for 3 months, then
back in basecamp one day
started bringing the lieutenant
his tray from the mess tent
and got transferred to the supply room
Kissed the war's ass goodbye

357 and a wake-up in the jungle
when the chopper came
and he said good-bye to the war

was climbing in
his steel pot already aboard, discarded
His head
full of tomorrows back in the world
When a sniper's bullet

Last Day In Viet Nam

It was either a sweep and mop-up operation
through the barracks of our last sleep in the Nam

or have our orders cancelled. One quick stroke of the pen
all that was necessary. Forget that freedom bird waiting.

For the pen, vowed the sergeant,
is mightier than the sword.

La Chingada

Alma Villanueva

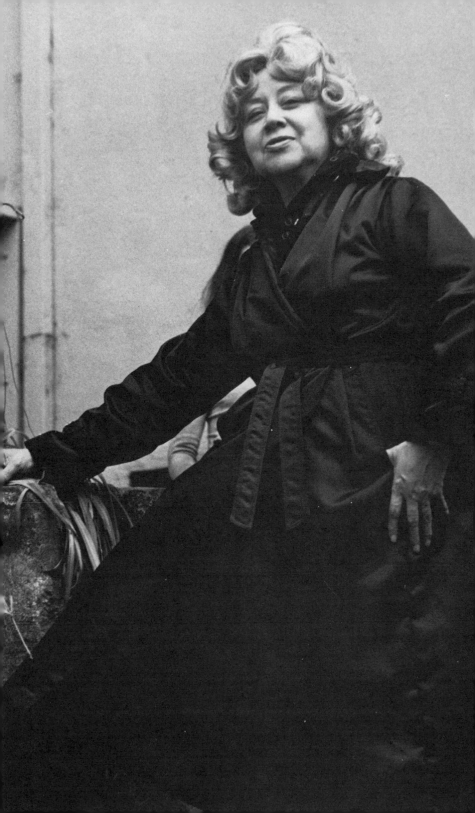

Alma Villanueva   Poetic and Autobiographical Statement

I think this poem may have been started with my great-grandmother Isidra, who was a missionary and healer in the early part of the century in Sonora, Mexico. She was a Yaqui Indian converted to Christianity and dared to name her daughter, my grandmother, Jesús. Then again, this poem may have started long before even Isidra, but I take great inspiration in that woman.

I feel that in physical and psychic history this poem goes back to the first discredited, the first raped woman—when the feminine was forced to abdicate its sacred power. In that moment the material, the matter, the mother, the flesh, the earth that bears us was denied its inherent sacredness. In that same moment Man believed he became pure spirit, thought—a strange, disembodied, masculine God—and he became utterly unloved, split and angry.

This poem is my furious response, centuries later, in our time, to the epitome of masculine culture. We begin to face the next century with the knowledge that the sacredness of *all* existence is now in danger.

I hope I also wrote this poem with a measure of tenderness for the sons who refuse to be "fathers," who begin to birth their feminine selves, who begin to love this earth.

My mother, Lydia, translated this poem at my request, but in many ways this is her poem—she is my mother. I felt her life as a girl, as well as my aunt's and my grandmother's, in my body, so really this is their poem. My mother, in translating this poem into Spanish, put it into her body and made it her own, and for that I am grateful.

I dedicate this poem to my newborn granddaughter Ashley—Ash-ley, who perhaps rises from the soft, silent ashes of women—and my baby Jules. Children of the new century.

Alma Villanueva, born in California in 1944. Author of *Bloodroot*, a collection of poetry, and a long narrative poem entitled *Mother, May I?* She won first place in poetry in the 1977 "Third Chicano Literary Prize" at the University of California, Irvine. Most recently the magazine *Metamorfosis* published a play, "The Curse," *Maize* a short story, "Her Choice," and *Beyond Rice* a series of broadsides in which her poem "Windy Women" appears. She also has an M.F.A. in writing.

Lydia Villanueva, born in Arizona in 1921. She is a pianist, lover of poetry, and medical secretary by profession.

Publications

Third Chicano Literary Prize. Irvine: University of California, 1977.

Bloodroot. Austin: Place of Herons Press, 1977; 2nd printing, 1982.

Mother, May I? Pittsburgh: Motheroot Publications, 1978.

"My Mecca" (poem). In *Hispanics in the United States: An Anthology of Creative Literature.* Ed. Gary D. Keller and Francisco Jiménez. Ypsilanti, MI: Bilingual Press, 1980. P. 110.

"Wild Pollen." In *Contemporary Women Poets.* Ed. Jennifer McDowell. San José, CA: Merlin Press, 1977.

"Legacies and Bastard Roses." In *I Sing a Song To Myself.* Ed. David Kherdian. New York: William Morrow & Co., 1978.

"To Jesús Villanueva, With Love" and three untitled poems. In *The Next World.* Ed. Joseph Bruchac. New York: Crossing Press, 1978.

"Windy Women." In *Beyond Rice.* Ed. Geraldine Kudaka. San Francisco: Noro Press, 1979.

"Golden Glass" (short story), "Siren," and "The Ceremony of Orgasm" (poems). In *Hispanics in the United States: An Anthology of Creative Literature. Vol. II.* Ed. Francisco Jiménez and Gary D. Keller. Ypsilanti, MI: Bilingual Press, 1982. Pp. 70-72; 101-03.

"The Love of It," "On Recognizing the Labor of Clarity," "A la vida," "Island." *ChismeArte,* I, 4 (1977), pp. 12-13.

"Pyramids and Such." *Somos,* Oct. 1978, p. 37.

"The Icicle." *Somos,* Dec. 1978, pp. 22-23.

"Myth of Isla Mujeres." *Somos,* April 1979, p. 11.

"Her Choice" (short story). *Maize,* Spring-Summer 1981.

"The Food" (prose) and "Bloodline." *ChismeArte,* Summer 1981. Special Women's Issue.

"Passion," "The Labor of Buscando la Forma." *Metamorfosis,* Spring 1982.

"Dark Roots." *Haight Ashbury Literary Journal,* I, 3 (1981).

From *Mother, May I?* In *Women Poets of the World.* Ed. Joanna Bankier. New York: Macmillan, 1983.

Life Span (poetry). Austin: Place of Herons Press, 1984.

La Chingada

"La *Chingada* es la madre forzosamente abierta, vio-
lada o engañada. Ella es la encarnación cruel de la
condición femenil."
                                        —Octavio Paz[1]

Primera Parte

(Las Vivientes)

¡No te dejes![2]   "Cada hija, aun en el tiempo antes de
Cristo, ha de haber anhelado tener
una madre cuyo amor para ella y
cuyo poder fuesen tan grandes que
pudiesen deshacer la violación y re-
gresarla de la muerte. Y cada madre
ha de haber anhelado el poder de
Demeter, la eficacia de su enojo, la
reconciliación con su ser perdido."
                                        —Adrienne Rich[3]

No hay mucho que diga
que sobrevivirás al nacer:
una criatura cruzando la boca
calle—el cuerpo enteramente
listo para correr al
otro lado, arropado en
ropaje caliente, cargando el
almuerzo a los cinco años—la
madre la preparó para este
viaje de cruzar la calle;
mira a los dos lados, luego
corre—y corrió con
toda la velocidad de un
millón de años de evolución.

Las cosas más simples requieren
la más grandiosa preparación:
un paseo por la playa solitaria
y fría—como me gusta

La Chingada

"The *Chingada* is the Mother forcibly opened, violated or deceived. She is the cruel incarnation of the feminine condition."

—Octavio Paz[1]

Part One

(The Living)

¡No te dejes![2]　"Each daughter, even in the millenia before Christ, must have longed for a mother whose love for her and whose power were so great as to undo rape and bring her back from death. And every mother must have longed for the power of Demeter, the efficacy of her anger, the reconciliation with her lost self."

—Adrienne Rich[3]

There's not much that says
you'll survive at birth:
a child crossing a busy
street—the entire body
ready to run to the
other side, swaddled in
warm clothing, clutching
lunch, about 5—the
mother prepared her for this
journey across the street:
look both ways, then
run—and she did with
all the speed of a
million years of evolution.

The simplest things take on
the grandest preparation:
a walk on the chill, lonely
beach—the way I like

a mí: camisa masculina de lana con
capucha, el perro, mi cuchillo abierto
y listo en la mano—una maestra de gimnasia
nos dijo 'si te atacan, no
    luches—hazte floja—es peor para
    las muchachas que luchan'—me supongo
que nos preparaba para todos
los paseos en el futuro.

Quisiera saber cuántas muchachas en
la clase se hicieron flojas, dejaron
la lucha—esto es de lo que
verdaderamente se trata, esta
preparación para el derrotismo, la
panza sumisa hacia arriba—en lo
salvaje, los lobos honran
eso: somos verbales—lo que
no se puede comprar o robar tiene
que aprender a ponerse en pie y luchar, o
correr, correr para salvar la vida.

Hay una pregunta aquí de
género, parece, un espíritu
infinito en el cuerpo de una mujer—
parece que he vuelto
al pavimento confinado, tierra
del hombre, tan cerca del
mar libre: tan cerca que yo
lo puedo ver y oler: yo
oigo a mi abuelita decir,
             'No te dejes'.

Un amigo mío me dijo una
vez, 'Los hombres tienen temor
de otros hombres, sabes—no estoy sin
    peligro solo'—las guerras pasan en
sucesión rápida: las gravideces
desperdiciadas, los dolores de parto
desperdiciados, las preparaciones
desperdiciadas: la preparación
de acero y muerte, el responder a

it: hooded, masculine parka,
the dog, my knife open in
my hand—a gym teacher once
told us 'if you're attacked don't
        struggle—go limp—it's worse for
        girls that fight'—I suppose
she was preparing us for all
the walks to come.

I often wonder how many girls in
that class went limp, gave up
the struggle—that's what it's
really about, this preparation
for defeat, the submissive belly
up—in the wild, wolves honor
that: we are verbal—what can't
be bought or stolen must
learn to stand and fight, or
run, run for
your life.

There is a question here of
gender, it seems, a boundless
spirit in a woman's body—
it seems I'm back
to the bound pavement, man's
country, so close to the
open sea: so close I
can see it and smell it: I
hear my grandmother saying,
        'No te dejes.'

A friend of mine, a man, once
told me 'Men are afraid of
other men, you know—I'm not
        safe alone'—wars flash by in
quick succession: the wasted
pregnancies, the wasted labors, the
wasted preparations: the preparation
of steel and death, to respond in
time to kill: the response is

tiempo para matar: la respuesta es
lo que vale—¿qué es violación? qué
es un asesinato cuando la tierra
está lista para tiro al blanco: del
satélite parece la tierra ser tan
redonda y pequeña: batimos como
recién nacidos tratando de respirar el
aire: corremos a la orilla de la centuria,
esperando llegar sin peligro al
cruzar.

Parece que aquí existe la cuestión de la
supervivencia: la cuestión de
reinventar el amor—principiar con la
tierra, lo que vemos es nada en
comparación con lo que sentimos: ve
dentro de ti—has vivido contigo
tantos años, no has rozado
la superficie del sentimiento, del
sentimiento: continúa—se extiende—toca
lo que el lenguaje nunca
alcanza, responde a un impulso
interno: nos recuerda que somos
pequeños y humanos, definidos
como tal, paro dentro de
una inmensidad giradora y en
rotación que responde a través de
estratos y estratos de evolución
y carne: anda por el
bosque, la próxima vez, examínate
tú: ¿vienen los animales salvajes
hacia ti o corren para salvar sus
propias vidas?

El amor es un sentimiento. El
amor conecta. Se nos olvida. Si
vamos a sobrevivir, nosotros
tenemos que crearlo mientras
caminamos, como cuando yo
camino por la playa sola,
diciéndome a mí misma que

what counts—what is rape? what
is murder when the earth is
divided neatly like so much
target practice: from a
satellite it seems so round
and small: we flail like
newborns grasping for air: we
run to the edge of the century,
hoping to make it safely
across.

There seems to be a question of
survival here: a question of
reinventing love—start with the
earth, what we see is nothing to
what we feel: tunnel in—you've
lived with yourself for so
many years, you haven't even
scraped the surface of feeling, of
feeling: it goes on—extends—it
touches what language never
reaches, responds to an inner
urge: reminds us, we are
small and human, defined as
such, but within
a whirling, spinning boundlessness
that responds through layers
and layers of evolution
and flesh: walk through the
woods, next time, gauge your
self: do the wild animals come
to you or do they run for
their life?

Love is a feeling. It
connects. We forget. If
we are to survive, we
must make it up as we
go along, like when I
walk the beach alone,
telling myself I belong

pertenezco aquí tanto como
cualquiera, cualquiera, cualquiera—
　'allí va un hombre—vamos
　a ver—cuál es su sentimiento,
　sentimiento, sentimiento—¿me
　violará, será él, será—
　será él humano hoy—
　reinventará el
　amor hoy? O
　me lo
　quitará'—
Me digo a mí misma 'no te dejes,
　dejes, dejes'—
él mira atrás una vez,
dos. Los dos
cruzamos al otro lado sin
peligro.

Tengo que decirles que es tiempo de
navidad ahorita, el tiempo del solsticio
de invierno, la luna es de
distancia cenital, el sol
discreto—las sombras
proyectan a lo largo,
fijamos la vista en la
sombra del otro—
se nos olvidaron los rituales del
invierno, el amor de
lo obscuro, el sueño largo—
algunos se asustan con
sus sombras. Ellos
acorralan venados silvestres
para la festividad, para que
los niños vean
el venado silvestre
de cerca, para que le den de comer
con sus manos nuestra
comida terrible que
nos causa la muerte—sólo
con ver una
cosa comparativamente primitiva

here just as much as
anyone, anyone, anyone—
    'there's a man—let's
    see—what's his feeling,
    feeling, feeling—will
    he rape me, will he, will—
    will he be human today—
    will he reinvent
    love today? or will
    he take it from
    me'—
I tell myself 'no te dejes,
    dejes, dejes'—
he looks back once,
twice. Both
of us make it safely
across.

I must tell you it's christmas
now, the time of the winter
solstice, the moon is
zenith, the sun
discreet—shadows
cast lengthwise, we
stare at each other's
shadows—we
forgot the rituals of
winter, the love of
dark, the long sleep—
some are frightened by
their shadows. They
pen wild deer for
the holiday, for
the children to see
the wild deer up
close, feed them from
their hands our
terrible food we
die on—just
the sight of a
comparatively wild thing

los induce a matar—'un
  venado acorralado fue herido hasta
  morir en una exhibición de navidad
  y una hembra preñada muerta a tiro de
  pistola en el parque local'—sus sombras
los alcanzan, los ciegan—sus estómagos
llenos de civilización, y mil
años de evolución—evolucionados
para sobrevivir sin amor o
hambre verdaderos, estos patéticos hijos
de mujeres. Matan para ver una cosa
silvestre morir.

Mis hijos, al fin, yo
les hablo a ustedes—
mis hijos—yo

les he enseñado a
soñar y hablar de
esto—yo

he llamado a la
niña dentro de
ustedes—los he hecho
vivir con
ella, con
migo (aunque no se puede
indicar exactamente—es
como debería de ser, sutil
e inconsciente como el latido
del corazón)—
ustedes soñarán todas las innominadas
ranas, gorriones, cangrejos de mar que ustedes
voluntariamente vieron morir (esto
siempre es parte de la jornada
masculina), pero ustedes los repararán
una y otra vez
en su sueño hasta que sus
cuerpos sean empreñados
con nacimiento—entonces
ustedes verdaderamente serán

drives them to kill—'a
  penned deer was stabbed to
  death in a christmas display
  and a pregnant doe shot in
  a local zoo'—their shadows
catch up, blind them—their stomachs
full of civilization, and a million
years of evolution—evoluted to
survive without love or
a real hunger, these pathetic sons
of women. They kill to watch a wild
thing die.

My sons, finally, I
speak to you—
my sons—I

have taught you to
dream and speak of
it—I

have called on the
girlchild inside of
you—made
you live with
her, with
me (though you can't put
your finger on it—it's
as it should be, subtle
as a heartbeat, unconscious
as such)—
you will dream all the nameless
frogs, sparrows, sandcrabs you
willfully watched die (this is
always a part of the masculine
journey), but you will repair
them over and over
in your sleep until your
bodies become pregnant
with birth—then
you will really be

hombres. Hombres
que amarán tanto
a la mujer fuera de ellos, como
a la mujer dentro de ellos y
probablemente uno al otro, la
tierra no puede esperar para siempre.
Es el tiempo de navidad, el cumple-
años de un hombre que permitió
que lo mataran (dicen)—
era el hijo de dios (dicen),
un hombre femenino que
abandonó la lucha,
dejando siglos de
obscuridad, una matriz sin
parto, abortos sangrientos
(llámenlos guerras)—hombres temerosos
de sus mismas sombras. Dejad
que estos hombres sean hijos
de la tierra,
de mujer,
que se abandonen
a sí mismos a
la nada. Dejadlos
reinventar el
amor.

Mi matriz ha sido penetrada con cohetes,
con cánulas de espacio, tratando de penetrar
el misterio de la existencia, tratando
de colonizar el planeta Venus, más caliente
que (supuestamente) el infierno: tú dices,
Venus puede derretir hojalata o plomo: yo digo,
mi matriz puede derretir cualquier forma extranjera
de vida. Venus está a salvo y sin peligro de ti
por ahora (sale de su concha y se eleva para
otro día de
amor).

men. Men
who may love
the woman outside them, like
the woman inside them—and
perhaps each other, the
earth can't wait forever.
It's christmas, the birth
day of a man who let himself
be killed (they say)—
he was the son of god (they
say), a feminine man who
gave up the struggle,
leaving centuries of
darkness, a womb without
birth, bloody miscarriages
(call them wars)—men afraid
of their own shadows. Let
these men be sons
of the earth,
of woman
that abandon
themselves to
nothing. Let
them reinvent
love.

My womb is pierced by rockets,
space probes, trying to pierce
the mystery of existence, trying
to colonize the planet Venus, hotter
than (supposedly) hell: you say,
Venus will melt tin or lead: I say,
my womb will melt any alien
form of life. Venus is safe from you
for now (out of the shell she rises for
another day of
love).

Parte Segunda

(Las Muertas)

1.

Pon esto bajo un microscopio.
Este papel es mi piel.
El primer error es el
de equivocar fuerza con
debilidad.
El segundo es el de
crucificarla. Y
el tercero es el de
adorarla. Cada uno

es un fracaso de madre,
la lección de vida de una madre.
Cada vez que te deja ir
cierta parte de ella siempre
se acuerda del infante inútil,
el desamparado
que moriría sin
ella, su
presencia; y ella creía en
el amor como en el salir del
primer diente, ella creía en
lo desconocido, la carne ensanchándose dentro
de ella, ella creía en
la suma responsabilidad—
el instinto la dirigía a cambiar el
curso, en lugar de eso decía
        'suéltate hoy', en
las palabras de sabiduría perdida,
las violadas del mundo
el linaje mudo de mujeres—
¡NO TE DEJES HIJA!

Es muy difícil pensar en las
violadas, todas las mujeres que
han conocido esa herida—
¿en dónde están sus gritos?

Part Two

(The Dead)

1.

Put this under a microscope.
This paper's my skin.
The first mistake is
to mistake strength for
weakness.
The second is to crucify
it. And
the third is to worship
it. Each

of you are a mother's failure,
a mother's lesson in life.
Each time she let you go
some part of her always
remembering the helpless
infant, the unprotected one
who would die without
her, her
presence; and she believed in
love as surely as the first
cut tooth, she believed in
the unknown, expanding flesh in
side her, she believed in
the utmost responsibility—
instinct guided her to turn,
instead saying
      'let go now,' in
the words of lost wisdom,
the raped of the world,
the mute lineage of women—
¡NO TE DEJES HIJA!

It is hard to think of the
raped, all the women that
have known that wounding—
where are their cries?

¿en dónde están sus sollozos?
¿sus iras estranguladas?
¿sus maternidades quebrantadas?
¿sus ternuras expuestas?
¿sus matrices forzadas?
¿sus cuerpos congelados para siempre
en sumisión? Aquí

en mis células lo he
cargado como un
cáncer, se da a nacer a sí mismo
asqueroso, deformado en la
página clínica. Deformado
porque cada hombre extraño
nunca sufrió su futilidad,
esto lo hizo una mujer: y luego
procedió a nutrirlo
silenciosamente, concienzudamente, maternalmente,

Yo desciendo hoy para invocar a las violadas.

"Hemos escondido nuestras hijas en cilleros—
nos han violado a todas, de la más joven a
la más vieja—riendo, gruñendo
haciéndonos sufrir más al
ver y escuchar a nuestros niños
gritar y llorar por
Mamá, Mamá, Mamá—yo
no creo que estos hombres
nacieron de mujer!"

Gritos obscuros.   Murmullos obscuros.

Palpitaciones obscuras.   Sangre obscura.

Entradas con melladura.   Carne forzada.

Piel muda lengua rebanadora.

Pies sujetos.   Manos sujetas.   Matriz sujeta.

their silent sobbings?
their strangled anger?
their crushed motherhood?
their tenderness exposed?
their forced wombs?
their frozen bodies forever
in submission? Here

in my cells I have
carried it like a
cancer, it births itself
ugly, deformed on the
clinical page. Deformed
because each alien man
never bore his futility, a
woman did: and then
she proceeded to feed it
silently, dutifully, maternally,

I descend now to call on the raped.

"We hid our daughters in cellars—
they raped us all, youngest to
old—laughing, grunting
making us suffer more to
watch and hear our children
scream and cry for
Mama, Mama, Mama—I
do not believe these men
were born of women!"

Dark cries.   Dark whispers.

Dark heaving out.   Dark blood.

Jagged entries.   Forced flesh.

Mute skin slicing tongue.

Bound feet.   Bound hands.   Bound womb.

Alma quebrantada.   El sexo femenino herido.

Ella anda errante por la orilla del río llorando
para siempre, lamentando y afligida por sus hijas
para siempre, inundando las riberas
para siempre, ahogando a los hombres.[4]

Valles violados.   Montañas asesinadas.

Desiertos desacatados.   Océanos aceitados.

Matriz de la tierra desperdiciada.

Canto de la ballena.   Lloro del somormujo.

Cuero del lobo, de la foca, del jaguar.

Despojado de uña, colmillo y garra.

Ríos condenados.   Hombres condenados a esta soledad furiosa.

¿DONDE ESTAN MIS HIJAS?
grita ella.
¿y mis hijos?
murmura ella, errante en la orilla del río
para siempre.
¡HIJOS DE LA CHINGADA!

2.

Madres asesinadas.   Hijas muertas.

Ya es tiempo. Ya es tiempo

de renacer virginales,
enteras e intactas. Ya es tiempo
de recobrar la salud de sus almas, de
la sangre y el calor de mi

matriz. Entren.
Entren cautelosamente, prudentemente, temblando

Slit soul.   Wounded womanhood.

She wanders the riverbank, crying
forever, mourning her daughters
forever, flooding the banks
forever, drowning men.⁴

Violated valleys.   Murdered mountains.

Desecrated deserts.   Oiled oceans.

Wasted womb of the earth.

Song of the whale.   Cry of the loon.

Pelt of the wolf, the seal, the jaguar.

Stripped bare of claw, fang and paw.

Dammed rivers.   Damned men to this furious solitude.

WHERE ARE MY DAUGHTERS?
she cries.
and my sons?
she whispers, wandering the riverbank
forever.
¡HIJOS DE LA CHINGADA!

2.

Murdered mothers.   Dead daughters.

It is time. It is time

to birth yourself virginal,
whole and intact. It is time
to heal your own soul, from
the blood and the heat of my

womb. Enter.
Enter shyly, cautiously, trembling

como lo hacen las mujeres, pero
entren. Yo

cargaré sus cuerpos delicados
este día. Es nada. Es
todo. Floten sin
esfuerzo. Duerman sin vergüenza.
Coman hasta saciarse. Yo escucho
sin oídos. Ustedes hablan
sin palabras. Somos una por
ahora. Hablamos el lenguaje de
la sangre.
La cuerda, el hilo que
siempre es cortado, repuesto por
aire fresco, y la lengua
trabajadora, la boca hueca, la
palabra ruidosa. Pero por ahora
somos una. La silenciosa simpatía de
matriz a matriz.

Parte Tercera

(La resurrección)

Rosa roja floreciendo sobre
la tierra: perfecta, dulce
gardenia de mujer, mi
hija, yo
misma nacida de
tierra y mujer: tu dolor
es el perfume de toda
vida: tu gozo
su canto: inviolada, tú
pertences a ti
misma: tus
brazos y piernas, perfectas: tu
sangre, perfecta: tu
corazón, perfecto: tu

as women do, but
enter. I

will carry your soft bodies for
this day. It is nothing. It is
everything. Float without
effort. Sleep without shame.
Eat to your fill. I am listening
without ears. You are speaking
without words. We are one for
now. We speak the language of
blood.
The cord, the thread that is
always cut, replaced by
cool air, and the laboring
tongue, the hollow mouth, the
noisy word. But for now we
are one. The silent empathy of
womb to womb.

Part Three

(The Resurrection)

Red rose blossoming upon
the earth: perfect, sweet
gardenia of woman, my
daughter, my
self born of
earth and woman: your pain
is the perfume of all
life: your joy
its song: inviolate, you
belong to your
self: your
limbs, perfect: your
blood, perfect: your
heart, perfect: your

matriz, perfecta: tu
alma, perfecta: tu
sexo femenino, perfecto. ¡O

sangre de la rosa, perfecta! ¡O
puridad de la gardenia, perfecta! ¡O
perfecta fusión! Yo
beso el vientre de Venus antes
que cualquier hombre.

¡O hijas de madres, vírgenes!
¡O madres de hijas, vírgenes!
Al fin, nacen a
sí mismas!

O tierra virgen de primavera, dame
tu obscuridad, tu riqueza—yo
sepultaré una pena antigua en
tu profundidad.

¡O tierra perfecta! ¡Escúchame!

¡Ella se eleva hacia la luz!

Translated by the poet's mother,
Lydia Villanueva

womb, perfect: your
soul, perfect: your
womanhood, perfect. O

blood of the rose, perfect! O
purity of the gardenia, perfect! O
perfect fusion! I
kiss your mound of Venus before
any man.

O daughters of mothers, virgin!
O mothers of daughters, virgin!
You are born, at last, unto
yourself!

O virgin earth of spring, give
me your darkness, your richness—I
will bury an ancient sorrow in
your depths.

O perfect earth! Hear me!

She rises to the light!

Notes

[1]From *The Labryinth of Solitude* (Mexico: Fondo de Cultura Económica, 1970).
[2]"To not allow oneself to die or be robbed or raped. to not abandon oneself."
Taken from *Appleton's New Spanish Dictionary*. (I added the word "rape" to the
definition.)
[3]From *Of Woman Born* (New York: Norton, 1976).
[4]La Llorona, like La Chingada, is one of the Mexican representations of
Maternity, Motherhood. La Llorona, "Weeping Woman," who wanders waterways
and towns at night, weeping and crying out, is a belief derived from pre-Conquest
times, when La Llorona was the Indian virgin earth-goddess Cihuacóatl. Taken, in
part, from Paz's *The Labryinth of Solitude*. The other manifestations of La
Llorona I heard from my grandmother.

La Isabela de Guadalupe
y otras chucas

Carmen Tafolla

Carmen Tafolla, born July 29, 1951, is a native of the west-side barrio of San Antonio, Texas. San Antonio is reflected in her work and in her soul.

She was educated through her elementary and junior high years in the barrio schools, from whence come many of her recurrent themes *(...and when I dream dreams)* and favorite characters *(Historia sin título* and *Los Corts 3).* In the 8th grade she received a scholarship to a private college preparatory high school, where she heard from her peers what the rest of San Antonio "knew" about the West Side. Walking home through her barrio, with the echoes of "You can't walk through the West Side without getting stabbed" in her mind, she began to comprehend the need for intercultural understanding. In 1969 she graduated from high school and proceeded to complete a Bachelor of Arts in 1972 and a Master of Arts in 1973.

In 1972 she compiled, for the Creative Arts of San Antonio Project, a collection of Mexican American folklore gathered from interviews with elderly Mexican Americans from her beloved West Side. These individuals provided the inspiration for later writings *(Los Corts 5, Ya No Voy Tomar).*

In 1973 she joined the faculty of Texas Lutheran College as Director of the Mexican American Studies Center. It was during her three years in this position that she began to publish her poetry and other writings. In 1976 she coordinated the Multi-Media Parent Training Packages Program at the Southwest Educational Development Laboratory and later served as head writer for *Sonrisas,* a nationally focused children's bilingual television series. In 1976 and 1977 she was selected nationally as one of the Outstanding Young Women of America. In 1977 and 1978 she was listed in the Dictionary of International Biography and the International Who's Who of Women, and in 1981 she was chosen by the Instituto del Lavorro i del Arte in Parma, Italy, as one of the Contemporary Personalities of 1981. In that same year she completed her Ph.D. in Bilingual Education.

Dr. Tafolla has publications in a variety of fields and has authored two high school textbooks, several articles, and six major screenplays for national television. Her book *To Split a Human: Mitos, Machos y la Mujer Chicana* was released in 1984. Her poetry has been published in numerous anthologies, and she is author of a book of poems entitled *Curandera* and an earlier co-authored volume entitled *Get Your Tortillas Together.*

The people of the barrios are the primary influence in her writings—what she calls "voice poetry." They are echoes of the voices of people whose lives are poems in action. And many center on San Antonio: the city's history, the city's spirit, the city's people.

In 1979 she married Dr. Ernest Bernal. In 1980 she became Vice-President for Operations and Chairman of the Board of Creative Educational Enterprises, a company they jointly founded to improve the quality of education for minority children. Presently she is Associate Professor of Women's Studies at California State University, Fresno. Her current projects include two novels, a TV miniseries, and a collection of poems, "From the Eyes of Guerilleras." She has four children—Ann Bernal (19), Sean Bernal (18), Cielos Tafolla Bernal (deceased), and Marilinda Tafolla Bernal (1).

Publications Related to Chicano Studies

Books

Get Your Tortillas Together (co-authored with R. Cárdenas and C. García-Camarillo). San Antonio, TX: Rifán Press, 1976.

Curandera. San Antonio, TX: M&A Editions, 1983.

Chicanas in the Arts (high school text). Washington, DC: Women's Educational Equity Act, 1984.

Chicanas in the Social Sciences (high school text). Washington, DC: Women's Educational Equity Act, 1984.

To Split a Human: Mitos, Machos y la Mujer Chicana, 1984.

Poems in Anthologies

Hembra. Austin, TX: Center for Mexican American Studies, University of Texas, 1976.

Travois: An Anthology of Texas Poets. Thorp Springs Press, 1976.

Using Contemporary Literature in the Classroom. Texas Circuit and Texas Commission on the Arts, 1977.

Dale Gas. Houston, TX: Contemporary Arts Museum, 1977.

El Quetzal Emplumece. Mexican American Cultural Center, 1977.

Canto al pueblo: An Anthology of Experiences, 1978. Eds. Leonardo Carillo et al. San Antonio, TX: Penca Books, 1978.

Beyond Awareness Curriculum. Austin, TX: ESC Region XIII, 1979.

Flor y Canto II. Albuquerque, NM: Pajarito Publications, 1979.

Women Working: Stories and Poems. New York: McGraw Hill, 1979.

Canto al pueblo, Arizona. Tucson, AZ: Post Litho Press, 1980.
The Third Woman. Ed. Dexter Fisher. Boston: Houghton-Mifflin, 1980.
Metis: Women and Their Work. Austin, 1981.
Album USA (11th grade text). Glenview IL: Scott-Foresman, 1984.

Poems in Periodicals

Caracol, Oct. 1975.
Tejidos, IV, 5 (1977).
Revista Chicano-Riqueña, III, 3 (1980).
Cedar Rock, Jan. 1981.
Southern Exposure, IX, 2 (1981).
Maize, IV, 3-4 (1981).
New Blood, Magazine #6, Boulder, CO, April 1982.
Revista Chicano-Riqueña, XI, 3-4.

Articles

"La Hispana." In *The New Ethnic Woman: Confronting Racism and Sexism* (a guide for teachers). Washington, DC: National Education Association, 1977.
"La Mujer Hispana." In *St. Paul Teachers' Manual for Multicultural Sex Roles Development.* St. Paul, MN: St. Paul Public Schools, 1978.
"El Cine Chicano." In *Conference Proceedings for El Primer Seminario Latinoamericano de Archivos de Imágenes en Movimiento.* México, DF: UNAM-UNESCO, 1980.
"Chicano Literature." *Texas Circuit Newsletter,* Vol. II, No. 1 (March 1980).
"Chicano Writing: Beyond Beginnings." *Southern Exposure,* Vol. IX, No. 2 (Summer 1981).
"A Review of *The Second St. Poems.*" In *La Red/The Net,* No. 83 (August 1984), pp. 4-6.
"From the Rio Chama to Zoot Suit: The Road to Mythical Realism." *The Pawn Review,* Vol. VII, No. 4 (June 1984).

I. La Isabela de Guadalupe y El Apache Mío Cid

La Isabela de Guadalupe y El Apache Mío Cid

I, as an India,
And you, as a Spaniard,
    How can we ever make love?

I, by mecate tied
    to a red dirt floor
    y una casucha de adobe
    en las montañas de cool morning
    and the damp of the wet swept floor.
Y tú, with your fine-worked chains
    Tied from armor to iron post.
    White stallions and engraved gateways
    And a castle of hot night,
    Fine tablecloth, and chandelier etiquette.
    And pierce-eyed thoughts
    From the noble-blooded soul.
    Rey en España,
    Hacendado en México,
    Y Emplumado Emperador entre los Aztecas.

Pero yo NUNCA FUI dese tipo!
En España, gitana
En México, criada
Y hasta entre Aztecas,
    yo no fui Azteca, sino obrera,
    cara triste,
    y calma.

I, que me gusta andar descalza,
y tú, bordado en hilos de oro,
    How can we ever make love?

Will I have to crawl inside your armor?
Will you have to paint your feet with dirt?
Will we have to stop the world, take off its reins,
and tell it to go ver si puso la marrana?

Have you ever seen mecate elope with chains?

Will we have to meet between the day and night,
enlazados, escondidos, entejidos en amor,
with two masks and jet-way tickets labeled "Smith"?

Will we make a funny pair—
        red dirt floor and chandeliers?

(Did we make that house already?)
Did we already shift the worlds,
blend over blend in prism states,
moving between the mirrors of our many, many lives?

Dime, ¿am I really the criolla en manta?
        ¿Are you really the apache in armor?
        Who did this for us already?
        Who gave my life to you to me to
        you and made it many-colored one?

I, as an India,
And you, as a Spaniard,
        How can we ever make love?
I as an India and?
—you as campesino and?
—I as la reina and?
—You as indito and?
—Yo la azteca and?
—Tú el tolteca and?
—Yo la poblana y?
—Tú Mío Cid y?
—Yo la mora y?
—Tú el judío y?
—Nosotros la gente y
        nosotros

la gente
y...
Amamos.

II. cobbled with mesquite blocks...

Caminitos

The pathways of my thoughts are cobbled with
   mesquite blocks
     and narrow-winding,
   long and aged like the streets of
     san fernando de bexar
       y la villa real de san antonio.
pensive
   y callados
cada uno con su chiste
   idiosyncracy
     crazy turns
that are because they are,
   centuries magic
     and worn smooth,
       still intricate.
cada uno hecho así,
   y with a careful
     capricho touch,
       así.

They curl slowly into ripples,
   earthy and cool like the Río Medina
       under the trees
   silently singing, standing still,
   and flowing, becoming,
     became
      and always as always,
       still fertile, laughing, loving,
       alivianada
   Río Medina,
     under the trees,
       celebrating life.

They end up in the monte, chaparral,
   llenos de burrs, spurs
     pero libres
   Running through the hills freefoot
    con aire azul,
   blue breaths peacefully taken
    between each lope
     remembering venado,
      remembering conejos,
     remembering
      where
       we came from.

Memories

Medina Magiadora
  My campmeeting-preacher grandfather
   used to wash souls here
    baptizing them
    in the name of.

  My fronteriza-fuerte great-grandmother
   washed clothes here
    scaring the stains away
    from her loved ones' clothes.

I only wash memories
  of lives and times I never knew
  Dipping them delicately
  in the soft waters of the shady
  Medina
  softly polishing them clean
  until the faces of the past are clear
    ...hello, great-grandma,
    in your 1867 norteña vaquero jacket
    and your tiny unconquerable
    face and frame.

...the frozen crisp image of a little boy
guiding log-laden mules
through the icy mountain morning,
dreaming of running far away
from his dead parents' graves,
dreaming of being far away
from the cold and the death...
...A bugler in the Civil war
who didn't speak English.
...Indian chicken-thief taking
out his anger on the small farms
around San Antonio,
taking his tiny brigade
on a joy-ride chicken-shout celebration
bareback around their civilization
taking what was his.
...A worried family offering a white horse instead
so Pancho Villa wouldn't take their youngest son
as soldier.
...A widow crossing an unimportant river,
later to become the Greenback-Wetback Curtain...
...A Basque street urchin flippantly jumping aboard-
ship for an unknown world
easy to conquer
in his young
pickpocket mind.
...una india, maidservant in the colonizer's house,
desired and daring, too efficient, too beautiful, too smart,
chased out after she bore his child,
alone but strong,
still studying, still too smart.
...quiet centuries of sailors and seashore dreamers,
quiet farmers, loud gypsies, songmakers and
                                        metalworkers,
maids, cooks, tutor-nursemaids, blacksmiths and
                                        woodcarvers
flow here from the ocean.
...star-scholars, hunters, potters, dreamworkers,
curanderas, earthworkers, drum-dancers,
sun-worshippers and river-followers
pour here from the land.

...vaqueros, fronterizos, rebeldes, and
as always, dreamers, poets
grow here,
breathe here now,
drinking from the waters
of the Medina.
Medina Magiadora.
Aquí estoy,
lavando mi herencia.

Los Corts (5 voices)

LOS CORTS 1 (LA MADRE)

Las dos de la tarde y el calor.
Sudor pegajoso saliendo hasta de los ojos.
Cuando yo era chamacuela, me encantaban estas tardes,
Porque podía ir a buscar los gatos del barrio dormiditos en sus
                                                              rincones.
Pero ahora es mija la que les va a buscar,
Sí, esos mismos gatos roñosos y flacos.
Y yo que ya no puedo respirar de tanto calor que hace en este
                                                              cuartito.
Me acuerdo de cuando era muy bonita—
Ahora el cuerpo se me va desbaratando cada día
Y la cara se va cayendo, y cuando lo arreglo
Parece de plástico, o de payasa.
¿Ya qué soy? Sólo sudor y dolores.
Uju—el bebito ya se despertó.
Mañana tendré que ir al welfare.
...Las tres de la tarde y el calor.

LOS CORTS 2 (EL CHAMAQUITO)

¡Jiiiii-jo! ¡Me jayé un daime!
¡Ta hueno eso!

Pa los airplanes que venden de wood
(¿O eran de cuara esas?)
Nuimporta—hasta los beisbol carts se compran a nicle,
(También esos dientes de wax...)
Cuando llega deri del trabajo, le voy decir,
O le asusto con los dientes.
Y esa vieja mala a la tiendita
que siempre me ta regañando,
Le voy *enseñar* ese daime
Pa que *vea*
Pa que *vea*...

LOS CORTS 3 (LA PACHUQUITA)

Oye tú—nomás no. La Silvia no vale nada.
Ta bien puta. Corriendo tras el Larry. Y él no la quiere. Yo sé—
porque me anda buscando a mí. He tol my brother.
Y después he asked me if I'd meet him a la tiendita afterschool.
Ta bien cool ese—ta pero *chulo*. Es
el más good-looking de to'a la class. Hijo, y el otro día,
traiba esa camisa azulita, con el collar p'arriba así,
y se veía su medallón en el chest,
y como siempre los zapatos shainados y el white hanky—
¡ta bien pacito!

Y La Sylvia piensa que lo va agarrar
—pero nomás con cadenas, muchacha—
porque anda tras esta aquí. Y yo no le voy correr.
Me dicen que she's gonna jump me,
pero tú no te apuras, manita—yo me defiendo.
Pinche puta, con la navaja se la entierro esas ideas. Yo me defiendo.
Porque nadie le insulta a La Dot.

...Ey—la Mary Pester le taba escribiendo
dirty notes a La Sylvia, y ella también patrás—
y taban diciendo malas cosas de Teodora. Me dijo Rosie.
Y que Manda y Rosie y la Teodora s'iban a juntar en P.E. para
dárselo a Pester y a Sylvia.
—¡You *bet*, muchacha! Aquí toy—lista!

Ajá, y a ver a quién más juntamos, porque La Sylvia
se junta con todas esas gordonas feotas que tan pero perras pa
                                                              pelear.
Sí, en las showers,
pa que no vea la Miss Hensley,
porque no le gusta que peleamos
en el gym floor.

LOS CORTS 4 (THE DROPOUT)

N'ombre, ya no voy.
Aunque 'buelita me diga.
Ese honroon teesher joto, pinche, caga'o
Ya no pue'e cerme *na'a*.
¡Porque yo no me dejo!
¿Y qué se creen?
Tan fufurrí y tan smart que se creen—
yo no soy tonto.
Pero me ponen las *hardest* questions—
Yo *no soy* tonto
¿Y qué m'importa?
Y qué m'importa si *soy* tonto—
¡mejor que ser *joto!*
They don' *like* me, y siempre acusándome a mí.
N'ombre, ya no voy.
Aunque 'buelita me diga.
(And I *wasn't* spikking Spenish.
I *wasn't!!*)

LOS CORTS 5 (LA VIEJITA)

Sí, entre, entre.
Usted es la que trabaja con El Padre Rodríguez. Pos la casa es
humilde, pero es suya. Para servirle, Teófila Hernández de Soto.
Soto, ese fue mi esposo. Sí, el de ese retrato allá—cuando éramos
jovencitos—reciéncasaditos—nomás teníamos el Benny Chuniar y
La Lupita. Uh—y la Lupita ya es grande—ya hasta se casó su *hijo.*
Ese es, sí, ese en el T.V.—cuando fue su gradu-ey-chón de jaiskul. Y
esa bebita ay en la mesita es mi nieta la más reciente, pero allí

nomas tenía los tres años, y ahora fíjate que ya tiene los siete. Sí, tengo mucha familia—digo, de los hijos y los nietos—porque ya de primos y de hermanos ya casi todos se han muerto. De hijos y de hijas tengo muchos, y nunca me dejan sola. Todos se han casado menos mijo el menor, Rudy (Rodolfo le puse, como mi hermano.) Ese es, el que está de uniforme de soldao. Sí, fue para Vietnam, y gracias a Dios, me lo mandaron bueno y sano otra vez. Nomás que me lo llevaron de muy muchacho y muy simpático y siempre sonriendo, y ahora a veces se me pone medio triste y se mete a pelear. Me dice que es porque le hacen menos y le insultan. Y dice que a veces es porque es mexicano. Y yo le digo que más antes, fue peor, y que su papá también tuvo que defenderse, ha sido así por mucho tiempo, que no se enoje.
Pero no puede hallar trabajo,
y, a veces, yo entiendo
y yo también me enojo,
pero nomás aquí adentro.
Aquí
adentrito,
y no le digo a nadien.

Dead Lipán Apaches

Dead Lipán Apaches shadow-shout through our streets,
on the rampage, angry spirits never dying
Even in you, once every six years,
"Ayeeeeeeeeeeeeeeeee!" and thundering happy hooves
raise dust behind them
on your civilized terrain.
   —Your composure you regain,
     And, civilized, sign their death warrants,
     once again.
     (never completely free from the echo
     of their shout, "Ayeeeee")

Silver-armored soldiers shoot them dead,
   keep shooting through the thundering corpses

But you and I both know
that when the visor's up
one can't see anything inside
except the inside side of armor.
—Only the soldiers are dead.
Lipanes, centuries gone, all still strong,
thunder stronger through our head
    —but you won't let them stop and chat,
        kiss, drink, be, make love

        so they just charge through,
        shouting mad.

    This time, I join them,
    thundering
    "Ayeeeeeeeeeeeeeeeeeeeeeeeeee!"

Cruel insulto

Cruel insulto que me arrojas
    con el dedo lento de tu corazón,

    entre mil insultos de tus serenos ojos
    buscando aliento en el horizonte
    mientras yo te ofrezco todo de lo más profundo—
    todo y retodo veces más.

Triste pensamiento que me dejas
    solitario y sin recurso

    que me agarra como compañera involuntaria,
    enloquecido, desesperado, víctima de su propio temor,
    mientras nos afronta sonriente la fría soledad
    que nos indicas sin palabra ni mención.

Seca noria de la esperanza que me sugieres,
    maldita ausencia de la vida.

Viejo nido del pasado que sólo grita fantasía,
fantasma, recuerdo muerto, y desolación
Que me chupa el jugo de las venas
Mientras oigo tu pisar en el polvo
de la distancia.

Allí por la Calle San Luis

West Side-corn tortillas for a penny each
Made by an aged woman
and her mother.
Cooked on the homeblack of a flat stove,
Flipped to slap the birth awake,
Wrapped by corn hands.
Toasted morning light and dancing history—
earth gives birth to corn gives birth to man
gives birth to earth.
Corn tortillas—penny each
No tax.

III. y se hincha into armor...

Bailar...

The comino morning sits down on the dawn
and breaks its desayuno con su taza de café.
Y yo, trapped between night and day,
Struggling to breathe my eyes open
Into a mind heating up with the sunlight
Mientras baila mi alma en cool sueños descansos de ti.

El mundo tiembla y renace por sus ojos,
Child and mother and father and seed, y luz.
Y tú, tan lejos que resfrías la casa,
Tan cerquita que te toco adentro de mis dedos.
En vuelos de música nocturna, juntos, locos, libres,
Bailo, abrasándote adentro de la almohada.

The sunshine peeks under the leaves of my eyes
Y se hincha into armor, as I wrestle with a heavyweight daylight.
Gana. ¡Qué pesado estar aquí sola sin ti!
Dogs singing at the moon now squint and curl to sleep.
I stagger out of bed, caddycorner to the floor.
The comino morning sighs, gets up, and goes to work.

Quisiera

Quisiera ver la luna besarte con su luz
    y la noche encobijarte tiernamente
    y las estrellas reflejar su gozo eterno en tus ojos
    y el sol amanecer con dedos dorados en tus labios.

Quisiera ver la brisa bronca de medianoche
    jugar con tus rizos de mar negro
    y bailar ruedas locas sobre tu cuerpo caliente
    mientras la oscuridad celosamente te cubre con su melena.

Quisiera ver tu sonrisa de sueños
    mientras la acaricia la luz de la mañana
    y poder sentirte despertar
    en los brazos calientes del miel de mi alma.

Pero las estrellas adoloridas y la pobre luna
    tendrán que esperar.
La noche sola y la brisa loca
    tendrán que esperar.
El triste sol y la mañana enamorada
    tendrán que esperar.
Y mis mil besos de amor para ti
    ¡tendrán que esperar!

At the Very Last Battle

The wooden rocking-horse in Reyes Cárdenas' yard
Sinks on bended knee like Chief Joseph
at the very last battle.

Staring into the ground and biting on its bit,
Saying "I am tired. My heart is sad and sick,
I will fight no more."

The only Mexican-American principal in Seguín
Waves a sad beer bottle at my Pacer
as it passes.

I drive up to my assigned parking space
And wonder if my lot is taken by the car next door
or if I really belong.

I turn the key and walk into the empty house,
Alone, like the rest of la raza,
a stranger in my own home.

Loca

Loca,
  loca soy
    loca melena derritiendo palabras y brisas
      lavándolas en el río.

    gitana coja soplando tempestad loca
      y chupándose los dedos después de sus mangos.

    gitana tuerta cantando a la luna loca
      y echándose unas polkitas con cualquierquestá
                                        enpantalones.

Loca, loca, de fantasma boca
que te escapan tus ojos
y te vuela tu troca.

loca,
loca cuna con motor y orquesta
llantas nuevecitas, la garantía sirve por un año.

loca colima pintándose la cara con zoquete
y pónte tu ombligo en el hoyuelo.

loca rodilla que se sangra y se dobla
y se cae sin amigos mientras te mueres de risa.

Loca, loca, de vestido de frijol
arroz en el molcajete
y blanquillos de mármol.

Loca,
loca soy
loca vela loca, prendida entre glaciares,
bañándose cada sábado con jabón de casa   en una
lágrima.

Esa casa ya no existe

"Me siento muy cansado," dijo el viejito barbón, y cerró los ojos
pa soñar otra vez.

"Ta loco," decía la hija, "Todavía habla de ir pa su país. ¿Y
cómo vas a ir? ¿A pie?"

"Ay, ya me voy pa la casa, pa ver a mis hermanas y los
compañeros que viven allí por mi calle. Y ese cura condenao que
me regañó. Y pa sentarme en la plaza por un rato."

Y la hija se reía, "¿No te acuerdas, viejo? Ya se murieron todas
tus hermanas. ¿Y cuál calle? Hace 70 años que te fuiste. Esa casa ya
no existe." Y salió del cuarto para atender a su quehacer.

Y el viejito todavía murmurando, "Sí me voy. Sí me voy ir. Pero ahoritita no. Porque la vieja 'ta muy enfermita y no la puedo dejar al momento....¿Vieja?...¿Vieja, estás bien?...Vieja, ¡contesta!" Y el viejo comenzó a sentirse muy mal. Y el viejo se acordó...."Pos ahora sí me voy. Ahora sí. Ya me voy. Ya me voy pa mi casa." Y la hija sacudía la cabeza, "No se le quita lo loco. Esa casa ya no existe." Y el viejito se quedaba con ganas de ir pa su casa.

Un día el viejito paró de murmurar y de pelear. "Me siento muy cansado," dijo el viejito barbón y cerró los ojos pa soñar otra vez. Y soñando con su casa, se fue pa su casa.

Pos, sí, la viejita enfermita ya se fue. Y el viejito barbón también se fue. Y hasta la hija mandona también se ha muerto. Y la casucha de mis abuelos se cayó.

Y a veces me siento cansada de trabajar y digo, "Ya me voy pa la casa." Y me siento a pensar, y me acuerdo que esa casa ya no existe.

IV. no me pueden chingar...

19 años

de niña fue pachuquita, valiente, chocante, peleonera,
y nadie le decía qué hacer.
nunca la habían conquistado.

a los 14 años la echaron de la escuela
pudiera haberse quedado
pero no se iba dejar
y no iba dejarle a nadie
            insultarla.
se quedó en la casa, ayudándole a mamá
            cuidando los hermanitos.
Se aburría. También pasaba mucho tiempo
en la esquina con Rudy y Mando, platicando, flortiando.
Mando tan chocante como siempre,
        Rudy tan dulce.
        (¡pero qué vato el Mando!)

a los 15 se puso pregnant. No supieron
sus padres. Nomás les decía que tenía
dolor de estómago. Querían mandartraer a
la Doña Chuchita, que se lo curara, pero ella resistía.
Tampoco le dijo al Mando. Alcabo qu'él ya se estaba portando
            bien frío
y pasando mucho tiempo con la hija de Marta Pérez. Una vez ella
se puso bien mal; perdió el bebito—así sin nacer el pobrecito.
    Pos mejor—que alcabo el pobre hombrecito no tuviera...
        Bueno... Nomás no tuviera.

Pasó un año. No salía mucho. Se quedaba en la casa pensando
de muchas cosas.
    Regresó el Mando. Quería verla en la esquina. Ella no quiso,
pero... fue. Con su carro nuevecito se creía muy chingón.
    Puro papel. —Ella no se dejó amadrear. Adentro se sentía bien

gacho—todavía dolía, pero no le dejó ver eso. Se hizo que no
le importaba—bien fresca. Ya comenzó a portarse bien feo él.
La 'staba lastimando. Comenzó a forzarla. Luchó pero él estaba
muy fuerte...
Regresó a la casa llorando.

A los 19 la conocí, trabajando en una fonda que ni era la más
limpia ni la más sucia. Recibiendo ni demasiados
ni muy pocos. Haciendo su salario.
Pasándola.
Tenía una fuerza y una mirada que le hacía más
mujer que la mayoría de las que ganan su
"respeto" en otros lugares. Otros
tipos de prostitutas
            Prostitutas elegantes, prostitutas respetadas,
            prostitutas del prestigio, prostitutas del dinero—
                presidentas de prostitutas, reinas de prostitutas,
                y toda la alta sociedad.

            Pero ella era más mujer—
                más mujer que todas. Ella vendía
                sus horas.
                Otras vendían
                sus vidas.

Me dijo:
            "Es que ya me cansé. Ahora—
            Nadie ma va decir qué hacer—nadie. Ahora tengo
            yo el control.
            Sí. Me hacen lo que les da la gana.
            Pero porque yo, yo digo.
            Yo decidí que iba dejarlos.
            Porque yo, yo dije.
            Por eso, me tienen miedo.
            Porque ellos chinguichinguichingui
            y a pesar de todo, saben
            que yo tengo el control final.
            Por tanto que me chingan de afuera,
                no me pueden chingar el corazón."

Terca

Te beso
   entre los dedos helados de mis rechazos
Te beso
   entre los dolores de mis cuerdas quebradas
Te beso
   entre las angustias de mi cariño que no muere
   y entre las vidas de mi calor inmortal.

Ni los desiertos quema-piel
  ni los glaciares mata-hombre
   me han quitado
    el sentir tierno
     que te tengo
    lo liviano de mis caricias
     de brisa secreta
    lo dulce de mis olas
     de deseo caluroso
    lo frío de mis siglos
     sin ti.

Te debo odiar
  Te debo ignorar
   Te debo olvidar
    Pero sigue el quererte acariciar
     Livianito como el viento
     Calientito como el sol
     Calladito como el cielo
     Hambrienta-loca-enterito
      como mujer
      en la simienza
      de su vida.
Te beso
  entre los pensamientos
    de mis días
Te beso
  entre las hambres
    de tu distancia

Te beso
　y te sigo besando
　siglo tras siglo
　　sin jamás poder
　　　sentirte otra
　　　　cosa que
　　　　　el puro
　　　　　　amor.

Como un pajarito

Mi tía tenía 71 años
Con trencitas blancas, hechas de historia y de inocencia,
Trencitas hechas a mano, hechas por su madre cada mañanita
　　a las seis de la mañana cuando la casa está
　　fría y sólo los pájaros se levantan.
Mi tía tenía 71 años y trencitas blancas.

Sus ojos cocinaban pan dulce y daban de comer a los niños.
Todos eran sobrinos. Todos eran mijito.
Chanclas en ritmo paciente venían a ayudar.
Una sonrisa de Pascuas y del almuerzo,
Dos hoyuelos llenos de susto, risa, y cinco años de edad,
Manitos de masa de tortillas.
Mi tía tenía 71 años y una vida de despertar a sus 6 de
　　la mañana, sus 6 apreciada.

　　　—Su carne helada,
　　　sus huesos pediches,
　　　la boca chueca, seca—dos dientes de
　　　piedra vieja.
　　　En cama desesperada hecha de
　　　trabajo y medicina agria
　　　. . . quejitas y suspiros—
　　　"¿Dónde estoy?"

...Un sueño de dolores y de memorias.
Una vida entera,
y una coma de días y de años.
—"¿Dónde estoy?"
...quejitas y suspiros,
Un perro asoleado y loco...
Hambre pesado en la cabeza...
Desconocido sentado en la veranda...
Sangre en la rodilla—"te caístes de la bicicleta.
   A la otra no te vayas tan lejos de la
     casa, ¿eh?"...
Pan bien quemado—qué lástima...
Tanto trabajo todavía y ya son las ocho de la noche...
Ya hice avena y no hay azúcar...
Me perdí en el centro. Ni pude hallar la calle
                 Comercio...
El dentista te va sacar todo, todo...
Gato roñoso, se le está cayendo la oreja...
Hace mucho calor, y esta lana picosa, esta cama y esta
                lana picosa...
   Casa vacía—todos están de vacación
            Menos yo.

Tía, ¿dónde estás?
...El invierno en las venas.
   Chanclas calladas—
     Pájaro sin canción.

Mi tía tenía 71 años.
Una quejita muy chiquita
   y se murió.
Una quejita de pájaro
   y cerró sus alitas.

Ya no voy tomar

"Ya no voy tomar"
dijo el tío en su cama de cruda.
"Ya no voy tomar"
dijo el tío amasándose los sesos.

Con un recuerdo nublado de una alegría bruta
Y música y risa y la guitarra de oro,
Y los ángeles en sus dedos
Y los cielos en su voz.

Y hermanos sin fronteras en la ola de la canción
Viajando juntos en el río de la vida y melodía
"¡Qué bruta la crudota que me di!"

"Y ya no voy tomar."

Y se fue con sus tortillas al trabajo,
al sudor, al patrón, al dolor
de la espalda y del insulto
y de la cárcel del dinero
Y se trajo sus diez pesos
al caer el sol.

Y solito, solitito se dirige a la cantina
pa juntarse con los compas
Y mañana sabe ya
que se levantará
con la melodía dulce
y "Ya no voy tomar."

Aullido eterno

The coyote moon nos envuelve in its howl
Su golden luz nos acaricia y nos mama.
Dicen que she's a sister of El Huitzilopochtli
Pero aunque la descabezaron, su cara guarda su corazón.

Flotamos en su amor de dedos frágiles,
Nos arrulla en la vejez de su canción,
Nos protege en la miel caliente de sus ojos,
Y nos asegura que siempre, siempre estará.

The coyote moon nos envuelve in its howl
And its howl
Es melodía dulce
Y amor eterno.

La Malinche

Yo soy la Malinche.

My people called me Malintzin Tepenal
The Spaniards called me Doña Marina

I came to be known as Malinche
    and Malinche came to mean traitor.

They called me—*chingada*
                ¡Chingada!

(Ha—Chingada! Screwed!)

Of noble ancestry, for whatever that means, I was sold into slavery
by MY ROYAL FAMILY—so that my brother could get my
                                    inheritance.

...And then the omens began—a god, a new civilization, the
                                        downfall of our empire.
  And *you* came.
        My dear Hernán Cortés, to share your "civilization"—to
                                            play a god,
    ...and I began to *dream*...
            I *saw*,
                and I *acted!*

I saw our world
  And I saw yours
    And I saw—
                    another.

And *yes*—I helped you—against Emperor Moctezuma Xocoyotzin
                                            himself!
  I became Interpreter, Advisor, and lover.
      They could not imagine me dealing on a level with you—
        so they said I was raped, used,
                        chingada
                        ¡Chingada!

But I saw our world
    and your world
    and another.

No one else could *see!*
      Beyond one world, none existed.
    And you yourself cried the night
    the city burned,
        and burned at your orders.
  The most beautiful city on earth
            in flames.
  You cried broken tears the night you saw your destruction.
  My homeland ached within me
            (but I saw *another!*)

Another world—
      a world yet to be born.
  And our child was born...
      and I was immortalized *Chingada!*

Years later, you took away my child (my sweet mestizo new world
                                                              child)
         to raise him in your world.
         You still didn't see.
            You *still* didn't see.
And history would call *me*
                     chingada.

But Chingada I was not.
   Not tricked, not screwed, not traitor.
For I was not traitor to myself—
      I saw a dream
      and I *reached* it.
             Another world...

                          la raza.

                    la raaaaaaa-zaaaaa...

Si escuchas el viento...

Si escuchas el viento nocturno
Que en respiros profundos te sopla
   —es que te lleva el mensaje
      de mi amor eterno para ti.

Si ves la luna gentil
Que acaricia su cielo moreno
   —es que te susurra el poema
      de mi amor eterno para ti.

Si sientes las estrellas festivas
Que explotan en alegría
   —es que te cantan la melodía
      de mi amor eterno para ti.

Y si te toca el calor de la noche,
O la frescura de la brisa,
O lo oscuro de las sombras,
O la luz de una sonrisa,
   —Sepa que sólo son mensajeros
   De mi amor eterno para ti.

Historia sin título

Una vez taba yo en el colegio y taba pero bien sura, man.
Me senté allí en la English class pa que me dijeran que yo no
sabía ni escribir ni hablar ni pa eso ni hasta escuchar. Y taba *bien*
sura, man.

Y me decían que este writer taba mejor que ese writer porque el
éste sí sabía cómo describir la gente como deveras eran—y me
decían de su "realistic quality" y me preguntaban que "do you see
that?" y yo que no veía nada. Y taba *bien* sura, man.

Y después nos ponían a write a theme, y que fuera un reaction al
realism del libro. Y yo que decía que no veía nada en el libro, y que
lo que era "real" era otra cosa. Pero me dijeron que el mundo
verdadero y el basic reality se veía en ese libro, y que lo que yo había
visto de la vida was unrealistic, unprofound, and not of the same
universal quality de lo de ese writer (el safao).

Y por un momento cerré mis ojos y pensé.

Y ya entendí.

Que ellos ni sabían lo que taba pasando porque they had
learned it de los libros que had learned it de los otros libros y nadie
sabía ni pensar.

Y ahora mi hermanita ta comenzando el junior college. Y le
andan diciendo las mismas cosas. Y se viene después de class con la
cara larga.

Y yo le digo que no se crea, pero ella dice que necesitamos "face
reality" y que nosotros tamos bien tontos.

Pero yo ya entendí.

Y se siente pero *bien sura*, man.

To Mr. Gabacho "Macho"

(an on-the-street response)

This is a different language, vato,
and you better learn it quick.
We're a talkin', Mr. Gabacho Macho
and you're scared cause I'm a spic.

You're hearin' and you're knowin'
and when it rains it pours
And just cause it's our English
doesn't mean that it is yours.

And you thought we didn't know it
and were "language disadvantaged"
And suddenly we're educated,
fluent, and de-savaged.

And there's words a pourin' out
that you never heard before
And they can't just all be Spanish
(like you learned once from that whore.)

There's words like ethnocentrism
and gross deracination
and eco-political hierarchy
and cultural exploitation.

And you're *sure* this isn't Pleasantville
or Smithville U.S.A.
Or Tom, Betty, and Susan's home
or even "Happy Days."

No, this isn't Middle America
or even upper lower...
...It's barrio town we're walkin' through
And your watch is runnin'
           slower.

There's hunger here and anger too,
and insult and frustration.
There's words you never heard about
like Gacho Agui-tay-shun.

No, Gacho isn't Macho
and we don't all carry knives
And our women don't all go to mass
nor our men all beat their wives.

Our men head more than welfare lines
And our women aren't so timid
And we don't steal fritos from your bowl
Or test Arrid to the limit.

Here "chili" isn't a dish with beans
It's a concentrated bowl of salsa
And my sister isn't pregnant
even though she *is* descalza.

The only sombreros I ever saw
were on the heads of tourists
and the girl with a rose between her teeth
is working as a florist.

And no, "te aguitaste"
doesn't mean that you drank water
And "Cuidao, porque me caliento"
doesn't mean it's getting hotter.

A project here's not what you *do*
It's where you *live*, and trust us—
when we talk about "los courts,"
we don't mean "centers of justice."

Sometimes you get the feelin'
we know this nation better'n you?
Well, Lordy me—how smart you be!
Cause that just might be true!

This is a different language, vato,
And you better learn it quick
Cause you see, Mr. Gabacho "Macho,"
This woman here's
      a spic.

V. San Anto'...

San Antonio

San Antonio,
    They called you lazy.
They saw your silent, subtle, screaming eyes,
    And called you lazy.
They saw your lean bronzed workmaid's arms,
    And called you lazy.
They saw your centuries-secret sweet-night song,
    And called you lazy.

San Antonio,
    They saw your skybirth and sunaltar,
    Your corn-dirt soul and mute bell-toll,
    Your river-ripple heart, soft with life,
    Your ancient shawl of sigh on strife,
        And didn't see.
San Antonio,
    They called you lazy.

444 Years After

(to Guadalupe)

If I gathered roses for you...
Like Juan Diego stumbling through the cactus,
wearing only calzones and faith
with his tilmantli,
    —I would smother them into
      my jeans jacket
      because I never had a tilmantli.

If I gathered roses for you...
(After all, it's still the doce de diciembre,)
But there are no hills on my block,
And the Bishop is *used* to miracles—
He's a Chicano,
    —¿would my jeans jacket sprout
      an embroidered vision
      of the same old Lupe
      with stars in her cloak
      but standing on a pick-up
      truck with melons?

If I gathered roses for you...
The prettiest and sweetest ones I could steal!
But all of them with a little note that says
"Me junté una docena,
pero nomás te traigo seis,
porque la otra media docena
se las di a mi querido,
con una canción y un poema,
y todo mi amor."
    —¿Would you understand?

    I think so,
    because despite what the Aztecs think,
    You're a Chicana too.

So 444 years from now,
I'll *still* gather roses for you.

(And for him.)

Paper Boy

She was the barrio's first paperboy
to be a girl,
hiding her hair under a cap,
shirted and jeansed in black stone eyes,
tuff with defense and survival.
Protecting her pocket treasure
with a *macana* made of steel pipe—
when they'd chase her
she'd curl around a corner
waiting through silent lung-booming breaths
for them to rush past,
as she swung at their knees.
Better than baseball
when you didn't end up
dead for your three dollar dowry.

Successful business-"boy"
until her cap could no longer suffice
to hide...
so she waitressed herself away,
too young,
and lied.
Slapping beer onto bar tables,
slapping arms away with a back onyx stare,
hiss the tip up into skirtpockets
and carry a *macana*
for different reasons.

Elegant beauty,
degreed and dressed,

B.S. in Business Management
(of course)
never wears a cap—nothing to hide—
tosses her head back and laughs
"If they'd known, in those days,
what child abuse was,
I'd a' been one...
As it was, I was called
a bad girl and whipped
with the belt buckle,
the soup ladle,
and everything else."

You flirt with her,
lean close and leer.
Her black pearl stare
macanas you to the wall:
She knows.
You curl inside your inner corners,
baseball, beer, and buckles aching,
breathlessly against the wall,
held captive by
the black
bruising
whisper
of
her eyes.

She walks away
taking her tip with a skirtpocket smile.
You know
that she knows.
    —you wanted to be a paper boy
        too, but man that you always try to say
        you are, you didn't
        have
        the guts.

Amarillo

(En la pisca...)

Con los ojos de mi llanto
Grito amarillo amargo.
Amarillo del sol que se murió
Amarillo del asco volteado en una sopa de no quiero
Amarillo de una tribu de limones
    piscando hombres verdes
        mujeres negras
        y niños castaños, con salsa.

Amarillo de un riñón
    con espalda lastimada
Amarillo del dolor
      que pega
    que abro mi boca
    y caen palabras amarillas, podridas,
        dientes amarillos, lengua amarilla, boca
        negra de gusanos,
    abro mi boca
        y cae silencio amarillo.

Grito amarillo sin boca
y veo amarillo sin ojos.
    La tribu está marchando amarillo
    y nos está tirando a la basura
    porque no sabemos amarillo
    y vivimos amarillo.
    Pero no vamos a morir amarillo.
    No vamos a morir amarillo.

El Chicano

Lo premian
    después de todo
    después de maldiciones
    y renuncios completos
    después de años
    y dolores e insultos
    después de úlceras
    y luchas casi-muertas.

Ahora lo premian
    en ceremonia formal
    con sonrisas y cristal
Lo laudan
    reconociendo ni la fracción
    de lo que ha hecho.
Lo premian—
    y le cae, al fin,
    el honor, y un poco de paz.

Lo acepta, da la mano, da las gracias,
    vuelve a la casa,
    lo contempla un momento
    y pues—
        lo pone en la mesa,
        lo olvida,
        toma su pluma otra vez,
        y comienza—
        a luchar por la raza.

Por los callejones

Por los callejones de tus desastres
  Y las banquetas rotas, chuecas de quebrado corazón

Pasa el hilo desconocido
  de un sentimiento
    suave y escondido

Es el amor
  que te sigue
  esperando calladito e incógnito
  que el día venga en que descanses
    en tu sonrisa.

And When I Dream Dreams...

when I dream dreams,
I dream of *YOU*,
Rhodes Jr. School
and the lockers of our minds
that were always jammed *stuck*
or that always hung open
and would never close,
no matter *how* hard You tried,
we messed up the looks of the place
and wouldn't be neat and organized
and look like we were supposed to look
and lock like we were supposed
                              to lock.

Yea that's right
I dream of *you*
degrees later
and from both sides of the desk
my dreams take place

in your two-way halls,
HallGuards from among us,
human traffic markers, bumps on the road
between the lanes,
to say, when we were supposed to say,
where to turn left, where right,
and how to get where you were going—
("You'll never get to high school
speakin' Spanish," I was told)
(nice of them, they thought, to not report me,
breakin' state law, school law, speakin' dirty [speakin' spanish]
and our tongues couldn't lump it
and do what they were sposed to do.
So instead I reminded others
to button buttons
and tuck shirttails in.)

I never graduated to a
Cafeteria Guard,
who knows how they were picked.
We thought it had something
to do
with the FBI
or maybe the Principal's office.
So we got frisked,
Boys in one line,
Girls in another,
twice every day
entering lunch and leaving
Check—no knives on the boys.
Check—no dangerous weapons on the girls
(like mirrors,
        perfume bottles,
            deodorant bottles,
                or teased hair.)

So we wandered the halls
    cool chuca style
    "no se sale"
    and unawares,
    never knowing

other junior highs were never frisked
never knowing
what the teachers said in the teachers' lounge
never knowing we were (supposed to be)
the toughest junior high in town.

And the lockers of our minds
are now assigned to other minds,
carry other books,
follow other rules,
silence other tongues,
go to other schools—
Schools of Vietnam,
Schools of cheap café,
Schools of dropout droppings, prison pains, and cop car's bulleted
brains.
Marcelino thought the only way
to finance college
was the Air Force
(G.I. Bill and *good pay!*)
War looked easy (compared to here)
Took his chances on a college education,
Took his pay on a shot-down helicopter
in a brown-skinned 'Nam,
with a pledge of allegiance in his mind
he had memorized through Spanish-speaking teeth
as a Hall Guard, "clean-cut,"
cut clean down in a hospital ward,
paralyzed below the lips,
that still speak Spanish
slowly.
Silvia thought no one had the right
to tell her what to do.
One year out of junior high, she bitterly bore
her second pregnancy,
stabbed forks onto café tables
and slushed coffee through the crowds
sixteen hours a day, and she was fifteen
and still fighting to say
"I HAVE A RIGHT TO BE *ME!*"
And Lalo with a mind that could write in his sleep

growing epics from eyes that could dream
now writes only the same story over and over
until the day
that it's *all*
over,
as he's frisked and he's frisked and he's frisked
and they keep finding
nothing
and even when he's *out*
his mind is always *in*
prison.
Like Lupe's mind
that peels potatoes
and chops *repollo*
and wishes its boredom was less
than the ants in the hill
and never learned to read because
the words were in English
and she
was in Spanish.

I wonder what we would *do,*
Rhodes Junior School,
if we had all those
emblems of *you*
stamped on our lives
with a big Red *R*
like the letter sweaters
we could never
afford
to buy.

I keep my honorary
junior school diploma
from you
right next to the B.A., M.A.,
etcetera to a Ph.D.,
because it means
I graduated
from you

and when I dream dreams,
—how I wish my dreams
had graduated too.

CHICANO POETRY:
A SELECTED AND
ANNOTATED BIBLIOGRAPHY

Santiago Daydí-Tolson
Ernestina N. Eger
Gary D. Keller

The bibliography which follows is divided into three parts. Section I is a bibliography of bibliographic material that relates to Chicano poetry. Each of the entries is annotated. Section II is a bibliography of articles, essays, introductory studies to collections or books of poetry, conference papers, dissertations and theses, newspaper articles, and allied materials that together comprise most of the general criticism and analysis of Chicano poetry. While the listing we provide is not exhaustive, it is fairly comprehensive. In addition, we have evaluated most of the substantive or more readily accessible entries. (Admittedly, two or three have escaped our annotative review, as have all the more ephemeral entries.) Finally, Section III presents all the published reviews or critiques that we are aware of to date about the five poets of Aztlán who are anthologized here.

I. Bibliography

Bruce-Novoa, [Juan]. "Selected Bibliography." *Chicano Authors: Inquiry by Interview*. Austin & London: Univ. of Texas Press, 1980, pp. 288-92.

> Forty-eight poetry collections plus ten anthologies that contain poetry are listed in this unannotated and unclassified bibliography of predominately book-length creative works.

Chicano Periodical Index. Boston, MA: G.K. Hall, 1981—.

Searchable by poet's name or literary genre, this bibliographic tool provides access to an increasing number of Chicano periodicals. Vol. 1 covers 1967-78, vol. 2 covers 1979-81, and subsequent volumes will be published as annual cumulations.

Eger, Ernestina N. *A Bibliography of Criticism of Contemporary Chicano Literature.* Chicano Studies Library Publications Series, No. 5. Berkeley: Univ. of California, 1982. xxi + 295 pp.

This unannotated bibliography includes 65 general critical sources on Chicano poetry as well as analysis and reviews of 99 individual poets. The bulk of the material is from the 1960s and 1970s. An earlier work by the same compiler, "A Selected Bibliography of Chicano Criticism," in *The Identification and Analysis of Chicano Literature,* ed. Francisco Jiménez (New York: Bilingual Press/Editorial Bilingüe, 1979), lists 60 items related to Chicano poetry. This bibliographer identified most of the sources included in the present annotated bibliography.

Lomelí, Francisco A., and Donaldo W. Urioste. *Chicano Perspectives in Literature: A Critical and Annotated Bibliography.* Albuquerque, NM: Pajarito Publications, 1976. 120 pp.

The authors of this essential research tool provide mini-reviews of 53 books of poetry published between 1939 and 1976. They also survey 14 anthologies which include poetry and, primarily through journal analysis, give many other sources of Chicano poetry and its criticism.

Martínez, Julio A., comp. *Chicano Scholars and Writers: A Bio-Bibliographical Directory.* Metuchen, NJ & London: Scarecrow Press, 1979. x + 579 pp.

At least eighty Chicanos who have published poetry are included in this directory. The *vita*-like format gives personal data, education, professional and/or community affiliations, honors, published and unpublished works, and criticism.

Ordóñez, Elizabeth J. "Chicana Literature and Related Sources: A Selected and Annotated Bibliography." *Bilingual Review/Revista Bilingüe,* 7, 2 (May-Aug. 1980), 143-64.

Forty-two book and poetry selections by 27 Chicana poets, 26 anthologies and journal issues containing poetry by Chicanas, and 27 critical articles are included in this research guide. It focuses on the 1970-80 decade, although one source dates back to 1955.

[Rojas, Guillermo.] "Toward a Chicano/Raza Bibliography: Drama, Prose, Poetry." *El Grito,* 7, 2 (Dec. 1973), 1-56.

Rojas' landmark bibliography comprises 48 pages of poetry citations focusing on individual poems from *movimiento* newspapers and magazines but also including 22 chapbooks and anthologies. Sponsored by the National Endowment for the Humanities, it was compiled by scanning the holdings of 20 Chicano Studies libraries in Arizona, California, New Mexico, and Texas. It covers 1965-1972.

Sonntag, Iliana. "Hacia una bibliografía de poesía femenina chicana." *La Palabra*, 2, 2 (otoño 1980), 91-109.

    This unannotated bibliography covers 27 Chicana poets, listing their books, poems published in anthologies and journals, recordings, and criticism of their work. It spans 1973-80.

Tatum, Charles M. *A Selected and Annotated Bibliography of Chicano Studies*. [Manhattan, KS: Kansas State Univ.,] Society of Spanish and Spanish-American Studies, 1976. 107 pp.

    Fifteen books of poetry written by Chicanos, 15 anthologies and journal issues featuring Chicano poetry, and 5 critical articles are cited and analyzed in the first edition of this work. A second edition was issued in 1979, increasing the entries in the preceding categories to 37, 22, and 18, respectively.

Treviño, Albert D. "Mexican American Poetry for the Secondary School Literature Program." *English in Texas* (Texas Joint Council of Teachers of English, Houston), 7, 4 (Summer 1976), 22-24. ED 134 986.

    Criteria of secondary school reading interest and maturity level, English language, and absence of taboo words were applied to select the 31 single works and 3 anthologies included in this annotated list.

Trujillo, Roberto G., and Raquel Quiroz de González, comp. "A Comprehensive Bibliography (1970-1979)." In *A Decade of Chicano Literature (1970-1979): Critical Essays and Bibliography*. Ed. Luis Leal, Fernando de Necochea, Francisco Lomelí, and Roberto G. Trujillo. Santa Barbara, CA: Editorial La Causa, 1982, pp. 107-82.

    One hundred fifteen books of poetry by individual authors and 31 anthologies containing poetry are identified in this unannotated list. Library of Congress call numbers are given for the 73 chap-books and 22 anthologies in the Univ. of California/Santa Barbara collection.

Zimmerman, Enid. "An Annotated Bibliography of Chicano Literature: Novels, Short Fiction, Poetry, and Drama, 1970-1980." *Bilingual Review/ Revista Bilingüe*, 9, 3 (Sept.-Dec. 1982), 227-51.

    Annotated citations are provided for 61 books of poetry by individual authors and 28 collections containing poetry.

II. Criticism

Aguilar, Ricardo D. "Chicano Poetry and New Places." *Journal of Ethnic Studies*, 5, 1 (Spring 1977), 59-61.

    Reflections on Chicano poetry in the Seattle area with samples of poetry by the author and by Gary Padilla.

Aguilar-Henson, Marcella. "Angela de Hoyos and Ricardo Sánchez: A Thematic, Stylistic, and Linguistic Analysis of Two Chicano Poets." Unpublished Ph.D. diss. Univ. of New Mexico, Albuquerque, NM, 1982.

Alegría, Fernando. "Chicanos: Introducción." *Hispamérica*, No. 2 (1972), pp. 37-39. Rpt. as "Poesía chicana." *Excelsior*, 10 marzo 1974, "Diorama de la cultura," pp. 5-6.

Brief and rhetorical glorification of Chicano poetry as the voice of rebellion against the capitalist system, namely the United States establishment. It equates Chicano literature and political upheaval with those of the Third World.

Bornstein, Miriam. "La poeta chicana: visión panorámica." *La Palabra*, 2, 2 (otoño 1980), 43-66. Tr. and slightly condensed as "The Voice of the Chicana in Poetry." *Denver Quarterly*, 16, 3 (Fall 1981), 28-47.

This major study gives a historical orientation to the poetry of Chicanas as well as specific attention to a number of poets including Bárbara Brinson-Pineda, Inés Hernández Tovar, Lorna Dee Cervantes, Margarita Cota-Cárdenas, Angela de Hoyos, Carmen Tafolla, and others.

Bruce-Novoa, John D. "Un análisis genérico de tres épicas chicanas." Paper presented at MLA, New York, 28 Dec. 1976.

On *Yo soy Joaquín*, *Perros y antiperros*, and *Los criaderos humanos*.

Bruce-Novoa, [Juan]. *Chicano Authors: Inquiry by Interview*. Austin & London: Univ. of Texas Press, 1980.

Includes poets Alurista, Abelardo Delgado, Sergio Elizondo, Rolando Hinojosa, Miguel Méndez, José Montoya, Tomás Rivera, Ricardo Sánchez, Tino Villanueva, and Bernice Zamora. Since these interviews were conducted by mail, each of the authors responded to the same questions, which included: What kind of book did you read in your formative years? Does Chicano literature have a particular language or idiom? What is the place of Chicano literature in U.S. literature? What are the milestones so far in Chicano literature? Who are the leaders among Chicano writers, and why? and many others. In this fashion, much useful information was generated and comparisons and contrasts across poets and other writers are made possible.

————. *Chicano Poetry: A Response to Chaos*. Austin & London: Univ. of Texas Press, 1982.

This book features close textual analyses of one Chicana poet, Bernice Zamora, and many of the best known Chicano poets including José Montoya, Abelardo Delgado, "Corky" Gonzales, Alurista, Sergio Elizondo, Miguel Méndez, Tino Villanueva, Ricardo Sánchez, and Gary Soto. Author's critical methodology makes use of the concepts of surface structure and deep structure from transformational, generative grammar.

Campa, Arthur L. "Protest Folk Poetry in the Spanish Southwest." *Colorado Quarterly*, 20, 3 (Winter 1972), 355-63.

Chicano protest folk poetry has a hint of humor and satire that are not characteristic of most protest, as defined by John Greenway in *American Folksongs of Protest.* Present-day protest folk poetry may be divided into the mostly traditional romance type poetry found in the Río Grande Valley and the more contemporary imitations of Anglo protest poetry found in the urban and semi-urbanized centers. Protest has been a traditional manifestation in Spanish literature and becomes endemic when the ills of society are chronic. The new Chicano folk poets differ from the traditional ones in having been raised in an English-speaking culture. They have lost the ability to use rhythm, rhyme, or metrical forms because they are more concerned with protest than with art.

Cárdenas, Reyes. "Chicano Prison Poets." *Caracol*, 1, 10 (June 1975), 3.

———. "Las Carnalas Poetas." *Caracol*, 2, 1 (Sept. 1975), 17.

———. "Crisis in Chicana Identity." *Caracol*, 3, 9 (May 1977), 14-15.

———. "Poetry Review." *Caracol*, 1, 7 (March 1975), 15.

Cárdenas de Dwyer, Carlota. "Chicano Poetry." *Literary Criterion* (Mysore), 12, 1 (Winter 1975), 23-35.

Written as an introduction for foreign readers who know little or nothing about Chicano literature, this article offers a very basic view of the subject. It stresses the fact that Chicano literature represents an "alternate tradition" within American literature. Viewed as a result of the Chicano political movement, Chicano poetry is defined by its social values; even its stylistic, thematic, and linguistic characteristics are explained as a consequence of a sociological factor—the homogeneous and self-enclosed Chicano readership. Alurista's work is discussed at length because of its representativeness.

———. "Chicanos: Their Prose y Poesía." *Review*, No. 13 (Winter 1974), 48-54. Revised version of "What is la literatura Chicana?" *American Pen*, 6, 1 (Winter 1974), 50-55.

A brief, general introduction for the novice.

———. "The Poetics of Code Switching." In *College English and the Mexican American Student*, Pise V. San Antonio, TX: Trinity Univ., 1977. Pp. 4-14. Paper presented at conference of same title, Pan American Univ., Edinburg, TX, 22 Jan. 1976.

Overview together with several salient examples of code switching in Chicano poetry.

———. "Poetry." In *A Decade of Chicano Literature (1970-1979)*. Ed. Luis Leal et al. Santa Barbara, CA: Editorial La Causa, 1982. Pp. 19-28.

A brief overview of the major works of poetry and anthologies of the decade.

Córdova, Robert Hernán. "Syntax and Bilingual Chicano Poetry." *DAI*, 38, 12 (June 1978), 7359-60A.

Using 100 bilingual Chicano poems, this dissertation attempts to establish the major lexical and syntactic characteristics of bilingual Chicano poetry.

Delgado, Abelardo. "Poetry as the New Source of Energy." *Caracol*, 2, 9 (May 1976), 7.

———. "Yo digo que..." *La Luz*, 3, 8 (Nov. 1974), 6. Also in *It's Cold: 52 Cold Thought-Poems of Abelardo*. Salt Lake City, UT: Barrio Publications, 1974. Pp. 76-82.
    Gives criteria for Chicano poetry.

Dickey, Dan William. *The Kennedy Corridos: A Study of the Ballads of a Mexican American Hero*. Austin: Center for Mexican American Studies, Univ. of Texas, 1978. 127 pp.
    An analysis of the *corridos* that emerged following the death of John F. Kennedy as well as an investigation of the state of the ballad tradition among Mexican Americans in the decade of the 1960s.

Flores, José. "Energía divina." *Caracol*, 4, 2 (oct. 1977), 9-11, 20. Response: del Bravo, Javier. In *Caracol*, 4, 4 (dic. 1977), 3.

de la Fuente, Patricia. "Themes and Trends in Chicano Poetry: Past, Present and Future." In *Reflections of the Mexican Experience in Texas*. Symposium sponsored by Texas Committee for the Humanities and Mexican American Studies Program, 19-20 April 1979. Ed. Margarita B. Melville and Hilda Castillo Phariss. Monograph No. 1. Houston, TX: Mexican American Studies, Univ. of Houston, 1979. Pp. 154-201. Commentary by Lucy Gonzales, pp. 202-07.

García-Camarillo, Cecilio. "Writing that Poem for a Chicano Magazine." *RAYAS*, No. 5 (Sept.-Oct. 1978), p. 3.

Garza, Mario. "Duality in Chicano Poetry." *De Colores*, 3, 4 [1977], 39-45.
    Starting from the premise that Chicano culture is subject to dualism such as Hispanic/Anglo and Spanish/Indian, the author discusses this element in Chicano poetry—for example, dualisms of English and Spanish, chaos and order, and so on.

Gonzales, Sylvia. "National Character vs. Universality in Chicano Poetry." In *The Chicano Literary World 1974*. Ed. Felipe Ortego and David Conde. Las Vegas, NM: New Mexico Highlands Univ., 1975. Pp. 13-28. ED 101 924. Rpt. in *De Colores*, 1, 4 (1975), 10-21. Response: Klor de Alva, Jorge. "Critique of 'National Character vs. Universality in Chicana [sic] Poetry'." *De Colores*, 3, 3 (1977), 20-24.
    Using examples of her own poetry, the author defends the idea that the Chicano poet, having already reached a sense of national identity, should evolve toward universal concerns. This is possible when the poet deals with individual experiences that become representative of the human condition in general. Adopting Vasconcelos' theory of the Cosmic Race, Gonzales explains how Chicanos, like all Latin

American people, are neither Eastern nor Western, but a combination of both through the Spanish and Indian traditions. The prophet or poet of the new race has yet to come.

González, Rafael Jesús. "Chicano Poetry: Smoking Mirror." *New Scholar*, 6 (1977), 127-38.

Utilizing examples from *I am Joaquín* and the poetry of José Montoya, Margarita Virginia Sánchez, Tino Villanueva, Luis Omar Salinas, and others, González investigates the issue of Chicano identity.

Grajeda, Rafael. "The Pachuco in Chicano Poetry: The Process of Legend Creation." *Revista Chicano-Riqueña*, 7, 4 (otoño 1980), 45-59.

A general historical introduction to the Pachuco and an analysis of this figure in the works of four Chicano poets: José Montoya ("Los vatos" and "El Louie"), J.L. Navarro ("To a Dead Lowrider"), Tino Villanueva ("Pachuco Remembered"), and Raúl Salinas ("A Trip Through the Mind Jail").

Hancock, Joel. "The Emergence of Chicano Poetry: A Survey of Sources, Themes and Techniques." *Arizona Quarterly*, 29, 1 (Spring 1973), 57-73.

In this survey the following thematic concerns are identified: the historical past and identification with indigenous cultures; allusions to figures and incidents related to the Mexican revolution; the life of the Chicano in the United States, emphasizing his oppression; the barrio; elements of Chicano culture such as food preparation and poetic evocations of family members such as *la jefita* or *los abuelitos;* and a call to social action through unity and solidarity.

Hernández, Guillermo. "Oral Composition and the Corrido Chicano." Paper presented at MLA seminar, Stanford Univ., 1975.

Herrera-Sobek, María. "Everywhere He Turns, the Immigrant Is Misunderstood: Here in the United States, as at Home in Mexico, Distortions Abound." *Los Angeles Times*, 21 May 1978, Sec. VI, p. 3. Analysis based on *corridos*.

————. "La imagen de la madre en la poesía chicana." Paper presented at conference on Women and Society in America, Univ. of California at Irvine and Casa de la Cultura, Tijuana, March 1978.

————. "The Theme of Drug Smuggling in the Mexican Corrido." *Revista Chicano-Riqueña*, 7, 4 (otoño 1979), 49-61.

An analysis of the thematics and moral messages in drug-smuggling *corridos* which, while they occasionally extoll the daring or cunning of the smuggler (sometimes seen as an anti-hero), typically express the moral value that "the wages of sin are death."

Hill, Patricia Liggins. "Roots for a Third World Aesthetic Found in Black and Chicano Prison Poetry." *De Colores*, 5, 1-2 (1980), 19-29.

Jackson, E. Beatrice Hathorn. "Chicano Thought in Chicano Literature." Unpublished M.A. thesis. Midwestern Univ., Wichita Falls, TX, 1971.

Johnson, Elaine Dorough. "Raza and Feminist Themes in a Selection of Chicana Poets." Paper presented at MLA, New York, Dec. 1978.

Leal, Luis. "Mexican-American Literature: A Historical Perspective." *Revista Chicano-Riqueña*, 1, 1 (verano 1973), 32-44. Updated version in *Modern Chicano Writers*. Ed. Joseph Sommers and Tomás Ybarra-Frausto. Englewood Cliffs, NJ: Prentice-Hall, 1979. Pp. 18-30.

An essay giving a historical perspective to Chicano literature, poetry included. Special attention is devoted to "pre-Chicano Aztlanense materials" such as the Hispanic period (to 1821), the Mexican period (1821-1848), the transition period (1848-1910), and the interaction period (1910-1942). The Chicano period is defined as beginning in 1943 with the Los Angeles Zoot Suit riots.

_____, and Pepe Barrón. "Chicano Literature: An Overview." In *Three American Literatures*. Ed. Houston A. Baker, Jr. New York: Modern Language Association of America, 1982. Pp. 9-32.

Lomelí, Francisco A., and Donaldo W. Urioste. "El concepto del barrio en tres poetas chicanos: Abelardo, Alurista y Ricardo Sánchez." *De Colores*, 3, 4 [1977], 22-29. Rpt. with English trans. by F. Lomelí and Sonia Zúñiga in *Grito del Sol*, 2, 4 (Oct.-Dec. 1977), 9-24 (Eng.) and 25-38 (Span.) Paper presented at AATSP, Chicago, 1975. Resumé in *Hispania*, 59, 1 (March 1975), 196.

Authors analyze how the themes of the barrio (seen as both an element of community and of personal identity) is developed in the work of these three poets.

MacIntosh, Roderick James. "A Comparative Study of French-Canadian and Mexican-American Contemporary Poetry." *DAI*, 42, 4 (Oct. 1981), 1625-26A.

Premised on a similar regional, isolated, linguistically different, and colonial status, this dissertation compares the thematic commonalities of contemporary French-Canadian and Mexican-American poetry. In particular, the qualities of protest poetry, the stylistics of literary satire, and the influence of North American literary trends are analyzed and compared.

Madrid, Arturo. "Social Tensions and Aesthetic Dimensions in Chicano Poetry." Paper presented at Popular Culture Assn., St. Louis, 20-22 March 1975.

Meléndez Hayes, Theresa. "Process in Contemporary Chicano Poetry." Paper presented in MLA, New York, 29 Dec. 1978.

Mirandé, Alfredo, and Evangelina Enríquez. "Images in Literature." In *La Chicana: The Mexican-American Woman*. Chicago and London: Univ. of Chicago Press, 1979. Pp. 142-201.

This important and extensive review surveys the image of the Chicana in American literature (beginning with the 1840s) and Chicano literature and contrasts these with the Chicana in Chicana literature. Citing scores of sources, the authors make the case that while Chicano (as contrasted to Chicana) literature is able to produce a range of characters who are truer or more credible, on the whole these achievements are governed by a masculine universe (as are the American works) which is limiting. On the other hand, despite its "lack of exposure" and "limited bulk, Chicana literature has probed deeper and more perceptively into the female situation and psyche than its American and Chicano predecessors."

Oberhelman, Harley D. "Pablo Neruda as a Precursor of Chicano Poetry." *Entrelínas*, 3, 1-2 (Spring-Summer 1974), 9-10.

Ordóñez, Elizabeth. "The Rebirth and Transformation of Chicana Poetry." Paper presented at AATSP, San Juan, 14 Aug. 1980.

Ortega, Adolfo. "Of Social Politics and Poetry: A Chicano Perspective." *Latin American Literary Review*, 5, 10 (Spring-Summer 1977), 32-41. Trans. as "Forjando una voz política en la poesía chicana." *Abside*, 42 (1978), 99-115.

Discusses the historical and social basis of the Chicano movement and its relationships with Chicano poetry. Once the first moment of enthusiasm has passed, the poet has to consider the alternatives of an art devoted to a larger and less exclusive political commitment. Gives some descriptions of different types of progressive Chicano poetry.

Ortego, Philip Darraugh. "Backgrounds of Mexican American Literature." *DAI*, 32, 9 (March 1972), 5195A.

Ortego, Philip D. "Chicano Poetry: Roots and Writers." *Southwestern American Literature*, 2, 1 (Spring 1972), 8-24. Rpt. from *New Voices in Literature: The Mexican American*. Ed. Edward Simmen. Edinburg, TX: Pan American Univ., 1971. Pp. 1-17.

Attempts to expose the cultural and historical roots of the Chicano people as developed by Chicano poetry, which is conceived as a new aesthetic in the service of these same cultural and historical characteristics.

Ortego y Gasca, Felipe de. "An Introduction to Chicano Poetry." In *Modern Chicano Writers*. Ed. Joseph Sommers and Tomás Ybarra-Frausto. Englewood Cliffs, NJ: Prentice-Hall, 1979. Pp. 108-16.

After establishing a context for Chicano literature that includes a history dating from 1848 (and, in a sense, prior to that date) as well as a geography that extends beyond the Southwest, the author introduces us to writers of the first half of the 20th century as well as contemporary Chicano poets.

Paredes, Raymund A. "The Evolution of Chicano Literature." *MELUS*, 5, 2 (Summer 1978), 71-110. Revised and expanded version in *Three*

220

Daydí-Tolson, Eger, Keller

American Literatures. Ed. Houston A. Baker Jr. New York: Modern
Language Assn. of American, 1982. Pp. 33-79.

Pérez. Arturo P. "Poesía chicana." Cuadernos Hispanoamericanos, No.
325 (julio 1977), pp. 123-31.

Defines Chicano poetry as an ethnic literature based within the
political boundaries of the United States. A poetry of social protest, it
reaches universality in its depiction of the injustices committed against
the Third World. The stylistic characteristics of this poetry (prosaism,
bilingualism, broken rhythm), the tone and attitude (despair, anger,
irony, enthusiastic call for action), and the themes are all consequences
of its being an art of social protest. This is a simple and basically
informative text aimed at readers unaware of Chicano literature.

Pérez, Wile. "Notes on Chicano Poetry." Caracol, 2, 2 (Oct. 1975), 16.

Pino, Frank. "Chicano Poetry: A Popular Manifesto." Journal of Popular
Culture, 6, 4 (Spring 1973), 718-30. Paper presented at Popular Culture
Assn., Toledo, OH, April 1972.

Relating the social and political conditions of the emergent
Chicano movement, Pino analyzes Chicano poetry as a popular
manifesto of the ideology and intentions of La Raza with respect to the
significant issues of the times. Three sources of popular poetry are
discussed: the ballad, the newspapers, and the creations of poets who
despite their individuality or professionalism still have roots in popular
lore.

Quintana, Leroy. "A Spark, A Raging Inferno, A Living Hell: Poems
from the New Mexico State Penitentiary." Agenda, 10, 3 (May-June
1980), 11-13, 21.

Rampersad, Arnold. "The Ethnic Voice in American Poetry." San José
Studies, 2, 3 (Nov. 1976), 26-36.

Ríos C., Herminio, intro. "La Voz Poética del Chicano." El Grito, 7, 3
(March-May 1974), 5-9.

Rodríguez, Joe. "Chicano Poetry: Mestizaje and the Use of Irony." Campo
Libre, 1, 2 (Summer 1981), 229-35.

Rodríguez, Juan. "El florecimiento de la literatura chicana." In La otra
cara de México: El pueblo chicano. Comp. David Maciel. México, DF:
Ediciones "El Caballito," 1977. Pp. 348-69.

Rodríguez del Pino, Salvador. "On Chicano Poetry." Xalmán, 1, 1 (July
1975), 11.

_____. "La poesía chicana: una nueva trayectoria." In The Identification
and Analysis of Chicano Literature. Ed. Francisco Jiménez. New York:
Bilingual Press/Editorial Bilingüe, 1979. Pp. 68-69.

A historical review beginning with colonial times and ending with
the poets of the nueva trayectoria. These are poets less directly
concerned with Chicano problems than their predecessors. Includes

brief references to some specific authors and a section devoted to Chicana poetry. Good introduction to a history of Chicano poetry.

Rodríguez-Puértolas, Julio. "Chicanos y corridos." *Papeles de Son Armadans*, 75, 224-25 (nov.-dic. 1974), 121-53. Rpt. as "La problemática socio-política chicana en corridos y canciones." *Aztlán*, 6, 1 (Spring 1975), 97-116.

Corridos, as romances, record history from the point of view of the people, the common man. Among Chicanos, corridos have long been a form of expressing their political and social complaints against the American system. This is mostly a selection of texts loosely connected by a thin ideological argument.

Sánchez, Ricardo. "Chicano Poetry: A Social Enigma." *Obras*. Pembroke, NC: Quetzal/Vihio Press, 1971. Pp. 11-34.

_____. "Introduction" [to Chicano poems]. In *From the Belly of the Shark*. Ed. Walter Lowenfels. Vintage 836. New York: Random House, 1973. Pp. 77-79.

Sedano, Michael Victor. "Chicanismo in Selected Poetry from the Chicano Movement, 1969-1972: A Rhetorical Study." *DAI*, 41, 4 (Oct. 1980), 1281-82A.

A study emphasizing the political aspects of Chicano poetry from 1969 to 1972. Analyzes the rhetoric as it expresses four dominant themes: the movement, the barrio, the Anglo, and the nature of Chicanismo.

Serrano, Estela S. "Introduction." *Montoya Poetry Review* (Sacramento, CA), 1, 1 (Spring 1980), i-iv.

Soto, Gary. "Reentrance: 4 Chicano Poets." *Revista Chicano-Riqueña*, 5, 4 (otoño 1977), 3-4.

Some personal observations about the book he edited, *Entrance: 4 Chicano Poets* (Greenfield Review Press, 1976), and about the work of Leonard Adame, Luis Omar Salinas, Ernesto Trejo, and Mario Chávez.

Tatum, Charles. *Chicano Literature*. TUSAS 433. Boston: Twayne Publishers, 1982. Pp. 36-48, 138-66.

A major landmark in Chicano criticism. In this book-length overview of Chicano literature, separate chapters are dedicated to the origin and evolution of Chicano literature (including poetry) from the 16th century and to contemporary Chicano poetry. In addition, contains a useful selected, annotated bibliography as well as a chronology of Chicano works.

Thompson, Lupita. "The Chicano Poet and Anti-Machismo." Paper presented at Popular Culture Assn., Pittsburgh, 27 April 1979.

Torres, Luis. "Relevance in Chicano Literature." *Metamorfosis* (Univ. of Washington, Seattle), 1, 1 (1977), 36-40. Paper read at Rocky Mountain MLA, Las Vegas, NV, 22 Oct. 1977. Abstract in *Rocky Mountain Review of Language and Literature*, 31, 3 (Summer 1977), 150.

Valdés Fallis, Guadalupe. "Code-switching in Bilingual Chicano
Poetry." *Hispania*, 59, 4 (Dec. 1976), 877-86. Rpt. from *Southwest
Language and Linguistics in Educational Perspective*. Proceedings of
the Third Annual Southwest Areal Languages and Linguistics
Workshop, Northern Arizona Univ., Flagstaff, AZ, April 1974. Ed. Gina
Cantoni Harvey and M.F. Heiser. San Diego, CA: Institute for Cultural
Pluralism, San Diego State Univ., 1975. Pp. 143-60. Discussion by
David William Foster, pp. 161-70.

    A study on sociolinguistics that uses poetry as a document for
linguistic research. Very useful for a better understanding of the
linguistic characteristics of Chicano poetry.

————. "The Sociolinguistics of Chicano Literature: Towards an
Analysis of the Role and Function of Language Alternation in
Contemporary Bilingual Poetry." Paper presented at MLA, New York,
27 Dec. 1976. Shortened version in *Punto de Contacto/Point of Contact*,
1, 4 (1977), 30-39.

    Analyzes Chicano English/Spanish code-switching both as a
mechanism for creating aesthetic delight in poetry and as an artistic
reflection of the same sociolinguistic phenomenon as it appears in
Chicano social communciation.

Vento, Arnold C. "Contemporary Chicana Poetry: 1969-1977." Paper
presented at Conference on Ethnic and Minority Studies (NAIES), La
Crosse, WI, 22 April 1978. Abstract in *Explorations in Ethnic Studies*, 1,
2 (July 1978), 81-82.

Villanueva, Tino. "Apuntes sobre la poesía chicana." *Papeles de Son
Armadans*, Nos. 271-31 (oct.-dic. 1978), pp. 41-70. Rpt. in *Chicanos:
Antología histórica y literaria*. Comp. Tino Villanueva. México: Fondo
de Cultura Económica, 1980. Pp. 48-67.

————. "Más allá del Grito: poesía engagée chicana." *De Colores*, 2, 2
(1975), 27-46.

    Engagée poetry differs from social poetry in that it requires the poet
to be fully involved in the social matters he addresses. Characteristics of
this type of poetry as exemplified by a Chicano poet from 1908 and by
contemporary poets who support La Causa are a spirit of
combativeness, the proposing of utopias, and a consideration of the
value of literature in the social movement. Two characteristic attitudes
are lament and confrontation. Engagée poetry goes beyond the simple
cry for justice. Innumerable typographical errors make the reading of
this article rather trying.

Yarbro-Bejarano, Yvonne. "*Teatropoesía* by Chicanas in the Bay Area:
Tongues of Fire." *Revista Chicano-Riqueña*, 11, 1 (Spring 1983), 78-94.

    Gives details about the emergence at the 11th Chicano Theater
Festival of *teatropoesía*, a fusion of these two genres.

Ybarra-Frausto, Tomás. "The Chicano Movement and the Emergence of a Chicano Poetic Consciousness." *New Scholar*, 6 (1977), 81-109.

In this paper, one of the most important to date, Ybarra-Frausto traces important historical moments of the Chicano movement such as the Plan de Delano of 1965, the Crusade for Justice (established in Denver, 1966), La Academia de la Nueva Raza (founded in 1969 in Dixon, New Mexico), and "El Plan Espiritual de Aztlán" and how a Chicano poetic consciousness emerged from the development of Chicano politics.

————. "The Popular and the Elite: Chicano Poetry." Paper presented at Latin American Studies Assn., Houston, TX, 2 Nov. 1977.

————. "Three Contemporary Chicano Poets: Antecedents and Actuality." *DAI*, 40, 6 (Dec. 1979), 3348A.

This study places Chicano poetry within a tradition extending back to 1848; it provides one of the first comprehensive views of Chicano poetry within a longitudinal sociohistorical context. In the second part of the dissertation, the literary production of three contemporary Chicano poets—Alurista, José Montoya, and Raúl Salinas—is examined within this sociohistorical framework.

Zamora, Bernice. "Archetypes in Chicana Poetry." *De Colores*, 4, 3 (1978), 43-52. Paper presented at MLA, New York, 28 Dec. 1976.

III. Criticism and Reviews

QUINTANA, LEROY

Kopp, Karl. Review of *Hijo del Pueblo. American Book Review*, 1, 1 (Dec. 1977), 19-20.

[Laird, W. David.] Review of *Hijo del Pueblo: New Mexico Poems. Books of the Southwest*, No. 235 (June 1978), p. 5.

Payne, James Robert. Review of *Sangre. Puerto del Sol*, 17 (Summer 1982), 127-28.

Waters, Frank, introd. *Hijo del Pueblo: New Mexico Poems*, by Leroy V. Quintana. Las Cruces, NM: Puerto del Sol Press, 1976. [P. v.]

TAFOLLA, CARMEN

Alurista, introd. *Get Your Tortillas Together*, by Cecelio García-Camarillo, Carmen Tafolla, and Reyes Cárdenas. N.p., 1976. [Pp. 4-5].

Cutting, Rose Marie, and Deanna Stevenson. "Texas Women Writers." In *Threads of Texas Literature: A Multi-Cultural Design. Essays Prepared for a Symposium on Contemporary Texas Literature, March 1-2, 1980, Thompson Conference Center, Austin, Texas*. Ed. Alison Heinemann. Austin TX: [Texas Circuit], 1980. Pp. 35-45.

Jensen, Ann L. "Poetess of the New Promesa: An Interview with Carmen Tafolla." *English in Texas*, Sept. 1981, pp. 17-19.

Vigil, Evangelina. "Una mordida de *Get Your Tortillas Together*, poesía de Cecilio García-Camarillo, Reyes Cárdenas and Carmen Tafolla (an analytic poem)." *Caracol*, 3, 9 (May 1977), 17.

See also entries by Reyes Cárdenas ("Carnalas" and "Crisis") and T. Mélendez Hayes in Section II.

VILLANUEVA, ALMA

Cody, James, introd. *Bloodroot*, by Alma Villanueva. Austin: Place of Herons Press, 1977. Pp. i-v.

Morales, Alejandro. "Terra Mater and the Emergence of Myth in *Poems*, by Alma Villanueva." *Bilingual Review/Revista Bilingüe*, 7, 2 (May-Aug. 1980), 123-42. Paper presented at MLA, New York, 29 Dec. 1978.

Ordóñez, Elizabeth. Review of *Bloodroot*. *Revista Chicano-Riqueña*, 6, 4 (otoño 1978), 75-76.